Praise for *The Chil*
Unhooking Custod

MW00605278

"At last, a sensible, smart, hones., ~....... book about child support: You couldn't find three more experienced, insightful, dedicated practitioners, whose description of the *disastrous* ways we have regulated child support is brilliant and spot-on. What is even better is that they have come up with a solution that actually prevents many of these conflicts and shifts the focus to the children. They have taken a giant step forward and deserve our immense gratitude. Their book is a life saver and a game changer–read it and buy copies for your friends."

Kenneth Cloke, JD, Ph.D. LL.M.
Director of the Center for Dispute Resolution
Co-founder of *Mediators Without Borders*

"At last, a truly groundbreaking, child-focused approach to support issues that will revolutionize how parents navigate children's expenses after divorce. Erickson, McKnight and Saposnek's 'Magnum Opus' describes with exquisite detail a game-changing new roadmap for how child support can and should be resolved. A must-read for all family mediators, other divorce professionals, and parting parents. Indeed, the most valuable book on child support published in the 21st century."

Michael Aurit, JD, MDR
President, The Academy of Professional Family Mediators
Co-Founder, The Aurit Center for Divorce Mediation

"Professional mediators Erickson, McKnight, and Saposnek have created a process where law and common sense can intersect. How rare! Their book, *The Child Support Solution*, is a must read for mediators, their clients, attorneys and judges. Long time advocates for children caught in the middle of a divorce fight, these experienced mediators have developed an intelligent model for divorcing parents to ascertain an appropriate amount of support for their kids. It takes the fight out of divorce procedures and focuses on the needs of the children, and how best the parents can meet them. Thanks to the authors for bringing their mediation experience to mitigate the stress of divorce."

Jocelyn Wurzburg, JD
First Professional Mediator in Memphis, TN
Civil Rights Activist

"This book offers an empowering and field-tested way for parents to put the needs of their children ahead of rigid Child Support Guidelines that so often pit parents against each other. It's a simple, practical idea–and also a radical innovation–that will improve the lives of parents and children alike."

William J. Doherty, Ph.D.
Professor of Family Social Science
Director of the Minnesota Couples on the Brink Project
University of Minnesota

"As a lawyer, therapist, and mediator, I have worked with many separated and divorced parents who end up fighting in court over incomes, earning ability, medical expenses, daycare, and even custody (to get a 'better' child support amount), because that's what the adversarial system encourages. With the use of the Child Support Account, in contrast, parents are more likely to cooperate, to keep the focus on the children, and to succeed at making their own plans for financially supporting their children–plans which they are more likely to follow. I heartily support this method of reducing conflict, over the use of state Child Support Guidelines."

Bill Eddy, LCSW, JD
Co-Founder and Training Director of the High Conflict Institute
Developer of the *High Conflict Personality theory*

"This book is a must read for students, parents, policymakers, mediators, and legal and mental health professionals working with separating families. It clearly defines a critical issue in family law that drives tremendous conflict between separating parents–tying child support amounts to the time spent with a child. The authors' proposed solution is simple, yet profound in its implication for shifting the focus in parent negotiations."

Connie Beck, Ph.D.
Associate Professor of Psychology
School of Interdisciplinary Arts & Sciences
University of Washington

"Many parents going through a divorce focus on paying or receiving child support based either on the advice of a family law litigator or on a computer program. This book liberates parents to focus on their children's needs for parenting and financial security. Authored by three of the leading mediators and parenting experts in the world, this book should be a first read for parents, divorce professionals, and the families and friends of people struggling to reorganize their lives."

Forrest (Woody) Mosten, JD
Professional Mediator
Collaborative Family Lawyer
Creator of *Unbundled Legal Services*

"While Minnesota 'non-court' family practitioners have been using Joint Accounts to separate parenting from child support for some time, Marilyn, Don and Steve have produced a marvelous book eloquently explaining in detail this breakthrough concept. It covers all aspects in a hands-on way. This book will help transform child support from an emotional conflict issue to one of parenting partnership for the benefit of children. Every professional and others concerned with divorce issues should own this book!"

Stu Webb
Trained mediator
Founder of the *Collaborative Law* concept

"*In The Child Support Solution, Unhooking Custody from Support*, Steve Erickson, Marilyn McKnight, and Don Saposnek, three of the most experienced family mediators in the world, offer professionals and parents a model to tailor child-related costs in separation and divorce to the parents' actual unique and changing financial realities. Rather than have child support costs determined by the amount of time (overnights) each parent has with their children, using state-imposed child support calculations for "average families" (that do not actually exist) and are difficult to change, the authors demonstrate how families can consider their children's actual financial needs to create a sensible plan for supporting their children, that is respectful, responsible and affordable."

Jim Melamed, JD
CEO, Mediate.com
Past Executive Director of the Academy of Family Mediators

"As a psychologist who specializes in trauma, I recommend this book, *The Child Support Solution,* for divorcing parents and all therapists and other professionals who work with parents who are dissolving their primary relationship. The approach described in the book minimizes the adversarial position that parents often get into as they attempt to divide assets, and it focuses the attention on what so often they can agree on, and on what will be required financially to support their child's well-being going forward in the manner they see fit. Given this change in focus–from giving money to an ex-partner to sharing in the cost of providing for children through the use of a joint account–it sets forth a clear directive, one that removes much of the potential for the ongoing conflict that creates a lack of safety for children as they transition to a new family life. I am confident that, if this model were to become the standard, the healing process of families in transition would be much kinder, gentler, and shorter, and would avoid the long-term consequences of combative uncoupling, whose effects show up in countless, destructive ways in the clients I have worked with over the past decades."

Susan Schaefer, Ph.D.
Licensed Psychologist
Co-Founder of the Midwest Center for EMDR Training and Therapy
EMDRIA Approved Consultant
Humanitarian Assistance Provider for the Trauma Recovery Network

"The Child Support Solution proposes an approach through which divorcing parents can agree upon how to address the financial needs of their children that is so practical and positive that it is hard to understand why it is not the law of the land in every state. Steve Erickson, Marilyn McKnight and Don Saposnek have created a gift to parents and professionals alike by describing, in step-by-step fashion, a creative, cooperative and collaborative problem-solving model for reaching a Child Support agreement that maximizes the ability of divorced or separated parents to meet the financial needs of their children in a positive and constructive way, while working within the limits that their divorce imposes on their individual financial resources."

Chip Rose, JD, CFLS
Past President of the Academy of Professional Mediators
National and International Trainer in Mediation and Collaborative Law

"This book is like a velvet hammer–an indictment of the current child support guidelines which then transitions into a new, logical, and non-threatening process to determine how children's expenses can be determined by parents who no longer live together. A very thoughtful and hard-hitting confrontation of the outdated family court practices, *The Child Support Solution* is grounded in the acknowledgement that court child-support guidelines discourage equal time-sharing. It provides practical solutions and reminders that parents can and will cooperate when they are allowed and encouraged to do so–outside of the family court system. The authors demonstrate how to really put the children's needs first, by abandoning the traditional child support guidelines in lieu of a process where the parents agree on "their own principles of fairness." This book opens the possibilities for a new way to do child support that makes sense for all mothers, fathers, and, especially, for children."

Molly K. Olson, M.B.C.
Founder, Center for Parental Responsibility
Co-Founder, Leading Women for Shared Parenting
Mediator, F.A.I.R. Solutions

"As a Certified Financial Planner™ Practitioner and Professional Family Mediator, I find this book to be groundbreaking. For the first time, it is letting parents be parents and not questioning what money is being spent on, and if it is going to the children. This is a great child-focused approach. Coming from the financial profession, it is the first time I have seen Child Support really make sense. It is a must read for divorcing parents. I plan on putting it on my recommended list of readings for all my divorcing clients."

Robert D. Bordett, CFP®, CDFA ®
Founder, Collaborative Practice & Mediation Services, Inc.

THE CHILD SUPPORT SOLUTION

Unhooking Custody From Support

Stephen Erickson, J.D.

Marilyn McKnight, M.A.

Donald Saposnek, Ph.D.

Published by
CSS Press

ISBN: 978-0-578-59744-7

Printed in the United States of America

> Details on discounts for bulk quantities of this book are available by contacting CSS Press at www.thechildsupportsolution.com

Cover design by www.milagraphicartist.com
Layout/production by Barb Frank: barbfrankdesign@gmail.com

Acknowledgments

This book is dedicated to all the parents who have chosen to deviate from Child Support Guidelines. They have thoughtfully decided to cooperate with each other and use the Child support Account, instead of fighting over limited financial resources.

Marilyn and Steve acknowledge the important work of their daughter, Solveig Erickson, M.S.W., who often is the first person that a client of ours in a divorce crisis may talk to. Her ability to calmly talk people off a ledge has been invaluable. More importantly, she has overseen helping create the specific core language of the Child Support Account needed in each mediation agreement in order to be accepted by the court. In addition, her editorial assistance with the developing drafts of this book has helped us shape the finished product into a useful tool for answering the frequently asked client questions that she fields each day.

Don further acknowledges all the children of divorce whose suffering, even in the best of parental partings, has taught us a lot about ways to minimize the financial and emotional damage frequently resulting from divorce. We hope this book will help relieve a good deal of their suffering, as their parents stop arguing and come together to truly support their children.

We also acknowledge the work of the many judges, mediators and attorneys who took a risk and helped normalize the successful use of the Child Support Account in those early days, by helping us finesse through the district courts a new and unknown approach to manage child support.

Most importantly, this book is also dedicated to that first mom from Edina, Minnesota, who, in 1983 said in a mediation session: "Why can't we each just put some money into one of our joint checking accounts to pay for the children's expenses? That way, the kids don't always have to ask me to get them everything."

Great ideas start with small steps.

Contents

Preface

After countless decades of observing the emotional and financial devastation resulting from on-going court battles over money and children, we confront a daunting truth–it is still the law in every single state in America that, following parental separation, the amount of time you spend with your children directly determines how much child support you will pay or receive. Moreover, the way for you to end up with more money is to get custody or more time with your children, or to restrict the other parent's time with the children. However, in spite of our current adversarial court system, where one side wins and one side loses, we no longer need to assume that separated parents will be in conflict over child support, or that they need to start court action against each other to determine the child support amount. We now have a SOLUTION to the need to engage in unnecessary battles over custody simply to obtain more child support dollars. Parents now can UNHOOK CUSTODY FROM SUPPORT.

It is time to recognize *both* parents as worthy and important to their children, regardless of their ability (or inability) to earn an income, and regardless of whether they spend more, or less, time with their children. It is time to recognize that divorcing parents need to be encouraged to concentrate on taking care of their children's needs, rather than on fighting costly and time-consuming battles in court.

For the sake of the countless children raised each year by separated or divorced parents, this book calls for a dramatic change in the way parents go about sharing the costs of raising them. We are now able to offer to courts, family law attorneys, divorce mediators and, most importantly, families, better tools to avoid these destructive contests.

In 1983, when we first offered our mediation clients the idea of a "Child Support Account" as an option for handling child support, most would say, "What a great idea! I like it!" We have described it to them in the following way:

As parents separate and divide their shared financial lives into two separate lives, they jointly decide on a budget that designates what they need to spend each month for their children's expenses. These may include such items as school lunches, clothing, activity fees, cell phones, health and dental insurance, and other expenses that they plan to share; the details of such a budget will be different for each family. Then, every month, Mom and Dad each deposit a pre-agreed amount of money into a joint checking account (their respective contributions may be in equal or unequal amounts), and both parents use the Account to purchase the budgeted items for their children. Because parents jointly create the rules for funding the Account and for spending from the Account, they become committed to follow the plan. They typically review their children's budget at least yearly and adjust their payments to the Account, accordingly. If the use of the Account proves unsatisfactory, either parent may terminate it at any time, and they will then be subject to the *Guidelines Child Support,* as set by the Court's formula for their particular state (each state sets its own formula for this calculation).

Using the Child Support Account in place of using the court-ordered Guidelines Child Support, changes the focus of the negotiations from "How much money will my adversary get from me?" to "How much money will our children need?" Most parents prefer using the Child Support Account in order to jointly figure out a monthly budget, discuss which expenses they can afford, and to see the money *go directly to the needs of their children,* rather than relying on the Court's Guidelines Child Support amount. When separated or divorcing parents become parenting partners and jointly create a plan for sharing the future expenses of their children, blaming and fault-finding are greatly reduced and, linking parenting time to child support in hopes of prevailing in money contests is eliminated.

With this explanation, our mediation clients proceed directly to the work of creating a budget of children's expenses and begin to discuss current incomes and future potential incomes. We strongly believe that the current Guidelines Child Support system is a disaster, with less than half (45.6%) of all custodial parents ever receiving their full amount of court-ordered child support[1] This results nationally in 114 billion dollars of arrears,[2] generating countless parental incarcerations, sanctions, and even a number of "Dead-Beat Dad Websites," showing mug shots of the worst offenders and listing the largest amounts of child support arrears! Our clients have decided to use the Child Support Account because it allows both parents to first create a budget of what it *really* costs to raise their children and to then make joint decisions about what they can and cannot afford.

Most importantly, upon hearing about the option for using the Account, parents instinctively recognize that it is worth a try, because it requires both parents to be engaged and supportive of each other in meeting their children's needs.

We hope that you will find this book to be a useful roadmap as you separately raise your children in a world of competing demands and uncertain economics. Using the Child Support Account will allow *you*–rather than the *state*–to decide on how to meet your children's important financial needs.

DISCLAIMER: Purchasers of this publication are permitted to use drafting language excerpts from this book in connection with agreements reached regarding child support and sharing of their children's expenses. While the authors and the publisher of this book have diligently used their best efforts to be accurate and complete in reporting their own experiences in connection with obtaining deviations from the Child Support Guidelines and court approval for using the Child Support Account with their own mediation clients, they make no promises, representations or assurances that these strategies will work for all readers of this book. Your own situation may be unique. However, we believe that, to be successful, parents must commit to be fair and equitable with each other, and thus, we strongly advise parents to use mediation, rather than litigation, in connection with resolving any conflict regarding sharing the costs of raising their children.

While we advise you to consult with other divorce professionals, where appropriate, this book encourages you and the other parent to avoid the excesses of the adversarial court processes, and to chart a cooperative course regarding the continued parenting of your children. As such, neither the publisher nor the authors shall be liable for any damages you might claim as a result of establishing or using the Child Support Account.

Finally, the footnotes of sources and website locations have been provided in an effort to offer to you additional resources. The reference material from the Office of Child Support and Enforcement is meant to be informative, and you are encouraged to read the "Essentials for Attorneys in Child [Support] Enforcement" if you reside in any jurisdiction that is prone to disallow deviations from the court's Child Support Guidelines. Readers should be aware that websites listed as sources or citations may have changed subsequent to the publication date of this book.

Introduction

In the United States, if you want to divorce, you must ask the court to dissolve your contract of marriage. Under "No Fault Divorce" statutes in each state, it is no longer necessary to show that one spouse's bad behavior caused the breakup; it usually is sufficient to provide a simple statement that declares, "There has been an irretrievable breakdown of the marriage relationship." However, there is more that you must do. In the divorce papers that you will submit to the court, you will also need to provide your agreements regarding the following four other specific aspects of your divorce:

1. **Property Division:** How you will divide property that is the result of the marital partnership.

2. **Spousal Support (Also called "Alimony"):** How each of you will begin to pay for your own separate living expenses, as you unhook joint monthly finances, upon separating. This is usually required when incomes are quite unequal, and when the higher income parent needs to help the lower income parent meet his or her expenses, for some period of time.

3. **Child Custody Determination:** (Also called and referred to in this book as "Creating a Parenting Plan"): How you will set up the on-going care and pattern of sharing time with your children after you separate.

4. **Child Support:** How child support was calculated using the state Guidelines formula, and showing who is paying it and who is receiving it (In this book, child support will be characterized as agreements that parents make regarding how *both* will *share* the costs of raising their children).

At the beginning of our divorce mediation practices in 1977, property, custody, and support usually followed a common settlement pattern, whereby mothers would be awarded the home, along with custody of their children, and fathers would pay child support and would be awarded visitation privileges by the court, which allowed them to "visit" their children every other weekend and Wednesday evenings. This was the pattern in virtually every state.

By listening to our clients over time, we learned that parents often objected to following this customary court-ordered path. Instead, they wanted to create their own principles of fairness and to deviate from what attorneys predicted would happen in court. A growing number of parents preferred more equivalent time-sharing of their children, so, Professional Family Mediators[3] moved from mediating "custody" to helping parents create a comprehensive "Parenting Plan." A number of parents also wanted to look at child support differently, eventually asking if it was possible to disregard the child support Guidelines and, instead, to use a joint account that each of them would contribute to and use to pay for agreed-upon shared expenses of their children.

The need for a different way to address the issue of child support grew, as more parents were living in close proximity to each other, sharing parenting responsibilities and sharing equitable time with their children. As a result of making decisions about their children jointly, both parents often took responsibility for purchasing items that their children regularly needed. Because of these changes, parents and professional family mediators found that the court's child support Guidelines no longer adequately served parents who:

1) engaged in approximately equivalent time-sharing of their children;

2) worked together in decision-making regarding their children's needs;

3) mutually participated in purchasing items for their children;

4) made an effort to live nearby each other;

5) did not view the other parent as either a "visitor" or an "adversary;" and

6) honestly tried hard to improve their communication with each other.

Currently, virtually all our new mediation clients with children choose to use the Child Support Account in their own divorce documents. As we have trained new mediators around the country and have introduced the Child Support Account as an option, mediators in other states have reported similar enthusiastic acceptance and successful use of the Account by parents who have adopted the method.

Partly due to the nation's changing economy, which now requires *both* parents to work full-time in order to survive, the U.S. has moved beyond the need to label only one parent as the primary, custodial, residential, psychological, and more-fit parent. And, perhaps, the time has come for you to shift your own long-held assumptions regarding child support from what is usually done, to what is possible!

An important note about terminology:

The states and the various jurisdictions within them use different designations to characterize the particular court that hears divorce cases. These include: *Family Court; Domestic Relations Court; District Court; Chancery Court; Probate and Family Court;* and *Juvenile and Family Court*; as well as others. For simplification sake, in this book, we will use the single term, "court", to designate the place in which a judicial ruling takes place for matters of parental separation and divorce. Similarly, the decision-maker in the court is variously referred to as a *judge; judicial officer; bench officer; magistrate; hearing officer;* or *referee*, as well as others. In this book, we will use the single term "judge" to describe the person who makes a judicial ruling.

Likewise, different states have different designations for the negotiated contract that ends a marriage. Depending on the jurisdiction of your divorce, this contract may be called a: *Marital Termination Agreement (MTA); Stipulation for Settlement; Marital Settlement Agreement (MSA); Decree; Judgment; Decree of Dissolution; or Judgment and Decree (J&D)*. In all states, it is the contract or legally-binding court order (based on the contract that you sign), that contains the terms of your settlement, concerning the four essential parts of a divorce (i.e. property division, spousal support, parenting plan, and child support). Interestingly, this document is the only contract you will ever sign in your lifetime that must first be pre-approved by a judge!

Additionally, throughout this book you will notice references to a variety of terms, child support formulas, and procedures, among the various states. This is because most divorce laws and procedures are the province of state law and can result in significant differences among states, depending upon whether, for example, you live in Kansas City, Kansas or Kansas City, Missouri. The only area of family law that is federal (and, therefore, uniform throughout the country) relates to the federal government's establishment of a nationwide system to collect child support arrears from all absent parents ("Absent" is the term used in the 1988 federal Family Support Act to refer to a parent who fails to pay court-ordered child support, resulting in the custodial parent seeking welfare). Since most welfare assistance in this country is funded by the federal government, Congress has a vital interest in ensuring that absent parents reimburse the government for unpaid child support. This is why large bureaucracies, called "Support and Collections" agencies, have been established in each state to track down and collect child support money from parents who do not pay their court-ordered amounts. Even if you are not an irresponsible "absent" parent, you still will likely be ordered to participate in mandatory wage withholding through Support and Collections in order to ensure that you make timely child support payments. Over time, this collection system has grown to include all divorces, even those in which no welfare is involved. This book shows you a plan for opting out of this elaborate bureaucracy, by creating your own child support rules in using the Child Support Account.

Chapter One:
Why the Child Support System is Such a Disaster

Considering the 114.6 billion dollars of unpaid child support owed in the US in 2017,[4] one would have to be naive to think that our current child support system is working well. Add to that the additional billions of dollars spent on child support hearings and on seemingly endless litigation, and with an estimated 50,000 men and women sent to jail each year for failure to pay court-ordered child support,[5] it is hard to deny that a big problem exists. Moreover, the significant cost of maintaining large agencies dedicated to child support collections in each state takes money away from families and taxpayers, and creates a draconian system of sanctions that has done little to solve the problem of how to share the costs of raising children in separate residences. Most importantly, this system has deprived countless children of a relationship with their non-custodial parent–most often their fathers–by using child support formulas that generate unnecessary custody battles and time-sharing disputes.

In 1998, we organized a small group of mediation colleagues to urge the Minnesota Legislature to change existing custody laws, for the purpose of encouraging parenting plan discussions in place of custody-contest preparations. The proposed change was similar to the changes sought by this book. As a direct result of our efforts over a two-year period, the Minnesota Parenting Plan Act[6] was passed in 2002, permitting parents to build parenting plans, thereby avoiding destructive custody battles. During our efforts to obtain passage of the bill, one Minnesota Legislator, who became a supporter of the bill, privately confided to us that almost a third of all calls to her office by voters in her district were to register complaints about the court.[7] She added that the majority of those callers expressed anger about and dissatisfaction with the way that *child support* was being handled. In addition to the bleak statistics about child support compliance, millions of co-parents carry on a negative relationship with each other that is often centered around child support conflicts after they divorce. The constant conflict and expense devoted to court appearances and collection efforts is mistakenly justified by a common misconception that so many of those divorced and unmarried parents are just high-conflict people who disregard their parental obligations; they are considered to be deadbeats, and, as such, there should be harsher sanctions for their failure to pay child support.

The child support problem is not about the parents who are the subject of court child support orders; **the problem is with the current court system and the false assumptions it makes regarding child support.** These false assumptions are rarely challenged, and as we examine them under the lens of critical thinking, we begin to question whether divorced and separated parents should even be subjected to a contest system for determining child support.

We believe there are five major flawed assumptions made by courts that continue to perpetuate this disaster. Operating by these false assumptions makes court the worst place to resolve child support conflicts. These assumptions are widely believed because they have become engrained into our thinking about divorce and separation. Understanding these false assumptions will make it easier to see what must be done to move beyond the present disaster that we call *The Child Support Problem.*

1. CONTEST MENTALITY – "The other parent is my opponent"

The legal system incorrectly assumes that parents who are not living together cannot cooperate with each other and must hold a contest in court to obtain resolution to their conflicts. Parents who enter the legal system are assumed to be "adversaries" in conflict just because they are in the midst of divorce. Their child support discussions and their subsequent interactions take place in the shadow of this contest mentality of the Court, making it difficult for them to reach agreement. Because of this incorrect assumption, couples without children, as well as parents, are required to have their divorce contract approved by a court that oversees an intricate system of rules of engagement between adversaries. Constructive, peaceful negotiations that create a support plan for their children cannot occur in this contest-environment that ultimately promotes winners and losers.

Constructive negotiations are severely hindered by this adversarial mentality, in which parents are encouraged to see the other as "the problem." The court system is unable to accept that most parents can find a sensible way (without court intervention) to share the costs of raising their children when living in two different homes after divorce. Instead, courts place parents in a coliseum setting, advising them to hire attorneys to help understand the rules of engagement so they can battle each other for more child support or fight to pay less child support. These contests have a high financial and emotional cost for all involved.

Because of this adversarial approach, attorneys representing individuals in court are obligated to *zealously advocate* for their client only ("zealously advocate" is the specific language used in most canons of ethics for attorneys).[8] Should an attorney try to help the other side or their children in the dispute, it could be seen as a conflict of interests, or as unethical. Not only does this contest approach create conflict residue that makes future co-parenting more difficult, it also limits most resolutions to only one of two results: either you receive child support or you pay child support.

A third option occasionally arises which could result in no exchange of child support, but in such cases, there is still a similar contest that centers around issues of trying to obtain (or reject) 50-50 time-sharing and trying to prove (or disprove) equal incomes in order to obtain the desired amount of child support.

The use of the Child Support Account does not require a "contest" to yield a solution, nor does it require a contest to decide who is the better parent. As such, it diverts the parents' focus away from the custody question towards finding a way to meet their children's living expenses. Setting up the rules for using the Child Support Account is an entirely different problem-solving process, that changes the game from who gets paid and who has to pay, to a new focus on an entirely different playing field with completely different rules.

This new direction takes parents down a more productive path in the search to find a way to meet their children's specific monetary needs regarding clothing, health insurance, tuition, summer camp, cell phones, etc. This work of jointly building the details of the Child Support Account requires face-to-face dialogue, rather than preparation for battle in separate attorneys' offices.

2. TRADING DAYS FOR DOLLARS – "More time with the child means more money for me"

In law review articles about child support, the linkage between winning custody to get more support is often referred to as "Trading days for dollars."[9] **The court system incorrectly assumes that a parent who has custody is the parent who makes all purchases for their children, and that is why that parent needs child support money.** However, it is not always true that having a child spend more time with a parent generates more costs. Other than food, almost all other expenses of children can be paid directly by either parent, and these costs, generally, are not tied to time with their children.

Except for situations involving equal timesharing, support formulas in all states designate the "custodial," or "more-time" parent, as the receiver of child support, because it is assumed that this parent spends more money on their children. However, this is not always true, and this linkage, unfortunately, creates significant negotiating problems. In some cases, it creates unnecessary custody contests, and in all cases, it tends to contaminate the negotiations regarding the parenting schedule. A parent who actually wants the other parent to spend more time with their children is often put in the untenable position of receiving less child support when the Guidelines are applied.

3. CHILD SUPPORT FORMULAS CANNOT ADDRESS IMPORTANT DIFFERENCES AMONG FAMILIES – A "One-size-fits-all" approach does not create fairness

Courts and lawmakers incorrectly take pride in the assumption that one single mathematical formula for calculating child support will produce universal fairness for families. A formulaic approach may be useful and expeditious for a judge who has to decide numerous child support cases each day, but a strict mathematical calculation does not address the specific expenses of all children–expenses that are unique to each family.

Most child support formulas consider only three things: **1)** Who has custody? **2)** What are the parents' incomes? and **3)** Are there any add-ons to be considered, such as health insurance or daycare, that might change the basic child support amount? These questions fail to take into account that child support is influenced by a host of other considerations, including housing costs, the children's ages, extracurricular activities, special needs, debts of the marriage, and unusually high medical costs of one or both parents.

4. PARENTS ARE NOT SURE WHAT THE "BASIC" CHILD SUPPORT PAYMENT IS SUPPOSED TO BE USED FOR – "What about extra expenses?"

Courts incorrectly assume that everyone understands what "basic child support" should cover. When only one parent is allowed to decide how to apply scarce child support dollars, confusion occurs when unexpected needs come up that are beyond food, clothing and healthcare.

Court-ordered child support is most often described as "basic" child support. This basic support is presumed to relate to the basics of living, such as food, clothing and other necessary living expenses for their children, but courts have not been explicit with the details of exactly how it is to be spent. Instead, they have trusted the custodial parent to make responsible choices. This lack of specificity has frequently created confusion and inter-parental conflict over what is supposed to be "covered" by the support. Parents have disagreed and fought over what each parent has considered to be necessary living expenses, including such items as cell phones, bicycles, enrichment activities, as well as a host of others. The flawed judicial assumption is that, after supervising a court-contest over the question of custody, parents, on their own, will cooperatively decide what child support is to be used for. Moreover, children *always* get caught in the middle when Mom says things like: "Ask your father to pay for your guitar lessons; I don't receive enough child support to pay for that." Then, days later after hearing the request, Dad says, "I am sending your Mother $835 a month for child support–you tell her that is what her child support is for." Many children, all over this country, are hearing these very words right now, as you are reading this.

The use of the Account also changes the parenting relationship for the better, by requiring the parents to create a more comprehensive listing of their children's expenses. Although, some existing state Guidelines may single out day-care costs and medical costs as shared additions to the basic child support award, other specific expenses of children are not included in most state Guidelines calculations. Guidelines formulas in use in every state do not need to consider, or detail, the actual costs of clothing, or clarinet lessons, or summer camp. The formulas only provide a lump-sum amount that the winner of the custodial battle will receive. The change in focus of the Child Support Account to the *details of the intended use of child support* not only eliminates confusion, but it also creates the structure that is so needed to move parents out of the initial turmoil of separation and divorce.

5. MOST PARENTS ARE NOT ABLE TO COMPUTE THE CHILD SUPPORT GUIDELINES, BUT THEY CERTAINLY ARE COMPETENT TO DETERMINE THEIR CHILDREN'S EXPENSES, AND HOW TO SHARE THEM

Perhaps the most far-reaching, and offensive, false assumption is that parents who are separated or divorced are no longer competent to determine for themselves how they will share the expenses of their children. The reality, however, is that parents have been determining how to meet their children's needs since the birth of their first child, and they will likely continue to try to do their best, if supported in that direction.

For too long, the thinking has been that, if parents cannot live together as husband and wife, then they can no longer raise their children together and that we must put one parent in charge of their children's lives and their expenses. This thinking is false because, even though a divorce can cause a good deal of stress, it does not permanently disqualify a person from being a competent co-parent. Moreover, starting to live separately should not disqualify one of the parents from participating in financial decisions regarding their children. The current system of child support Guidelines and rigid, court-ordered, sanction-driven child support is demeaning to the intelligence and good will of millions of divorced parents who are trying hard to cooperate with the other parent.

These five flawed assumptions have produced very profound and far reaching problems, primarily affecting the children, who are also marginalized when a system creates two classes of parents: one "absent parent" and one "custodial parent."

Despite the good intentions of courts and lawmakers, existing laws regarding child support Guidelines continue to produce high rates of non-compliance. Since passage of the 1988 Family Support Act that required each state to establish child support Guidelines systems "to collect money from the absent parent,"[10] states and the federal government have found it necessary to create new enforcement tools that serve as sanctions against parents who fail to pay their court-ordered child support.

The Federal Office of Child Support Enforcement informs visitors to its website what it can do to ensure compliance with the child support award:

> "The child support program works with both parents to collect consistent, timely child support payments. When child support is not paid regularly, we can take actions to collect monthly and past-due amounts. These various types of actions can affect the parent's finances, mobility, and public record and include:
>
> - Income-withholding;
> - Levy financial accounts;
> - Intercept a state or federal income tax refund;
> - Withhold other one-time or recurring federal payment, such as retirement, salary, payments to vendors or contractors, and other federal payments;
> - Deny a passport;
> - Suspend licenses (driver's, occupational, and recreational);
> - Set liens on property;
> - Report child support debts to credit bureaus." [11]

This is not a comprehensive list of sanctions. However, when a parent gets behind in child support payments, the court can send that parent to jail for contempt[12] or for the felony crime of non-support,[13] as well as charge up to 12% interest on unpaid child support in some states.[14]

Despite all the above sanctions, the magnitude of problems created by the false assumptions of the existing child support system continues:

a) The 114.6 billion dollars of uncollected child support (as of April 2017), reported by the Office of Child Support and Enforcement,[15] continues to increase each year.

b) The estimated 50,000 (and possibly up to 90,000) parents incarcerated each year for "criminal non-support" or contempt of court for failure to pay support (the exact number is difficult to calculate, due to the fact that no national statistics are kept on types of offenders in county jails)[16] constitute a true debtors' prison of enormous proportions. Not only are parents who go to jail unable to work off the child support arrears while incarcerated, but they find it difficult to obtain work upon release because they are now either felons or have spent time in jail for contempt of court and must disclose such information on all future employment applications.

c) The "loser" in the adversarial contest is often labeled a "non-custodial," "non-residential," "non-primary," "non-psychological," "visiting," "Disneyland," "absent," and/or "deadbeat" parent.

If we are a nation of laws, we must ask the threshold question, "Why is it that so many parents do not comply with state child support laws?" We have concluded that, too often, we look for solutions on the battlefield of the court "contest" system, rather than in the hearts of the parents. If children really are our primary concern, we must begin to apply critical thinking and examine the role that the court plays in driving families further into conflict and driving parents and their children to become alienated from each other. The real answer to the question of why there is poor compliance with child support orders is that the system, more than the parent, is at fault.

If we expect separated parents to effectively co-parent their children, we must move beyond rigidly relying on child support Guidelines because use of these formulas has created millions of unnecessary custody conflicts in their attempts to calculate the "legal" child support amount. We must move beyond creating a contest over who is in charge and toward helping each parent realize that they are BOTH in charge. We must give these parents the tools for learning how to cooperate and work together to jointly provide for their children, especially regarding child support–*One of these tools is the Child Support Account.*

Reform efforts to change the contest have been only mildly effective

Since the 1970s, small steps have been taken by courts and legislatures to try to make divorce less conflictual. The move to "no-fault" divorce in the 1970s made property division easier to resolve, and the move in the 1990s to replace "custody and visitation" decisions with the notion of developing "parenting plans," helped reduce the need for custody contests. However, child support remains a source of conflict, producing many unnecessary custody court battles and contributing to unending inter-parental conflict after divorce. Courts are at a critical juncture and need to employ new approaches to better manage the post-divorce expenses of children.

1. PROPERTY DIVISION HAS BECOME LESS CONFLICTUAL UNDER NO-FAULT DIVORCE LAWS. Before the 1970s, under "fault divorce," most states' divorce laws provided for an unequal division of property, awarding less property to the person who was shown to have caused the marital breakdown. By the end of the 1970s, most states had passed laws that did not punish the so-called wrongdoer. These new "no-fault" divorce laws eliminated the need to show one person at fault and, generally, called for an equitable (read: "more equal") division of marital property regardless of who might have "caused" the marital breakdown. Not having to prove fault, or defend against fault, was welcomed as an improvement, because the property division became more a function of determining asset values and deciding who wanted which items, and then equalizing the overall amount between the spouses.

2. CUSTODY HAS BECOME MORE ABOUT NEGOTIATING A PARENTING PLAN, AND LESS ABOUT ENGAGING IN A CONTENTIOUS CUSTODY CONTEST. Since the early 1980s, professional family mediators have urged parents to direct their money and energy away from the custody battle and toward negotiations for building a parenting plan. This has resulted in many parents creating detailed agreements that contain a calendar of time-sharing schedules, and specific plans for such matters as residential arrangements, communication protocols, joint parenting rules at both homes, school decisions, extracurricular activities, and transportation of their children, to name a few.

3. ALTHOUGH CHILD SUPPORT GUIDELINES HAVE BEEN ADJUSTED IN VARIOUS WAYS OVER TIME, THEY STILL CONTAIN ALL OF THE FLAWED ASSUMPTIONS DISCUSSED ABOVE. Past attempts at improving the child support system have been limited mainly to changing the Guidelines formulas or adding more sanctions for non-compliance. The Guidelines have also been changed by adding various items, such as healthcare and childcare costs, onto the basic child support calculation. And, almost all states have adopted what is called an "income shares" approach; this is seen as an improvement, because it considers both parents' incomes, rather than only the non-custodial parent's income.[17] In 2008, Minnesota joined the majority of states in using the "income shares" approach, instead of calculating child support based only on the non-custodial parent's income. The switch to consider both parents' incomes was seen as more fair, because it followed a proportional approach requiring the higher income parent to contribute more toward the expenses of their children than was required of the lower income parent.

While these attempts at improving the Guidelines can be applauded, the adjustments still did not change the basic framework of the adversarial contest system. Flawed thinking is still present; the contest still impacts the negotiations; and parents still get caught up in the undertow of the adversarial negotiations or litigation. As Bill Doherty, Professor of Family Social Science at the University of Minnesota and a member of the Minnesota committee working to move divorce out of the court system, has observed: "Contest-thinking is baked into the current divorce system."[18]

The combination of continued flawed thinking and failure to find ways to make child support decisions less contested has created a perfect storm, making the current method for calculating child support ripe for major reform. Unfortunately, trying to tweak the Guidelines formulas or creating harsher sanctions are not the answers. The only answer will be found in a completely new approach–that removes the contest and asks the parents to focus primarily on their children's actual expenses and how they might directly share them.

The Child Support Account is that New Approach

The current "System" of adversarial divorce will always generate conflict. Resolving the conflict over child support requires a completely new approach, one that changes the task from *engaging in a contest to developing a plan*. Since the late 1980s, we have seen how using parenting plans defines a new future and creates a new relationship between parents, by encouraging them to let go of past conflicts and embrace better decision-making regarding their children. Use of a parenting plan results in parents creating a "business-like relationship," based upon their future shared responsibilities for their children. Likewise, creating and using a child support plan is the next step in helping separating and divorcing parents to move away from an emphasis on contests, that are based on fault, toward an emphasis on future financial planning for their children's needs.

In order to see the destructive impact of the contest system, Table 1-1 highlights the dramatic differences between the Legal System's view of parents and the Child Support Account's view of parents:

TABLE 1-1

Legal System's View of Parents	Child Support Account's View of Parents
1) **Irresponsible:** Parents cannot be trusted to act responsibly in caring for their children's needs.	1) **Responsible:** Most parents try their best to meet their children's needs in a responsible way.
2) **Incompetent:** People who are not lawyers are not competent to decide child support. Navigating the child support Guidelines is complex and requires the assistance of a lawyer.	2) **Competent:** Most parents are competent in managing their children's expenses. Child support can be viewed as a planning process, not a legal process.
3) **Unlikely to Comply:** Divorced parents need strong Child Support Laws and strong sanctions to make them comply. The child support laws exist to force irresponsible parents to support their children. They make it difficult to deviate from the law.	3) **Likely to Comply:** Only a small percentage of parents intentionally reject the obligation to support their children. Parents need to learn about all their options concerning child support alternatives that are based upon trust and mutual responsibility.

4) **Likely to Default on Their Court Ordered Obligations:** Courts must confiscate the child support from a payor's wages to ensure that it gets paid. Not requiring wage withholding only hurts women, who are more likely to be the custodial parents.

5) **Only One Parent Pays for Children's Expenses:** The custodial parent always spends more for the children. That parent deserves child support from the non-custodial parent. Besides, if they cannot live together as husband and wife, how can they possibly be expected to raise their children together in two separate homes? We must, therefore, put one of them in charge and have the visitor send money to the custodial parent.

6) **Parents Need Strong, Zealous Advocates to Legally Represent Them:** Each side in the contest needs strong attorneys to separately provide them with legal advice, if forced to pay the child support, and legal advocacy to obtain the child support they are entitled to receive.

7) **Parents Need Certainty, Therefore Changing Child Support Should be Made Difficult:** The custodial parent needs certainty about the money that parent will receive as child support. The court should make child support difficult to modify, so that a sense of finality can be achieved.

8) **The Child Support Account Will Only Work for A Minority of Parents,** because parents cannot be counted on to carry out such plans on their own. Divorced parents need strong enforcement mechanisms to ensure their children receive money from the non-custodial parent.

4) **Unlikely to Default When Jointly Creating the Plan:** Most parents hope to be successful when voluntarily paying into a joint account managed by both parents. Banks will accommodate payroll transfers to the Account. If a parent does not pay, the Child Support Account can be terminated, and Support and Collections can take over management of child support.

5) **Both Parents Can Pay for Children's Needs:** The assumption that the custodial parent will spend more money on their children has created the mess we are in. It has established two classes of parents; custodial and non-custodial parents. Time with a child does not dictate who spends what on their children. With the exception of food, other children's expenses need not be tied to time shared with their children.

6) **Parents Need Effective Guidance:** Parents need to know all their options regarding child support methods available. They can do this by learning about the pros and cons of all options: The Guidelines; the use of the Child Support Account; and the benefits of employing a professional, client-centered, family mediator, who has the interests of both parents and their children in mind.

7) **Parents Need Flexibility, Because Incomes Change, and Expenses of Children Will Change Over Time:** Parents need a system for modifying child support, when necessary, without the need to return to court.

8) **The Child Support Account Has Been Shown to Work Very Well,** and will continue to work well for parents who are willing to try to build a constructive relationship with the other parent.

Chapter Two:

Change the Game from a *Contest* to a *Plan*

In order to successfully create and effectively use the Child Support Account, attitudes of each parent towards the other parent need to change. Fortunately, professional family mediators have found ways to help change attitudes by urging parents to take a mutual view by framing problems as common sense tasks rather than as legal issues, by changing the questions that are typically asked in divorce, and by using different words, terms, and concepts.

Change the Game by Beginning to Think Mutually

When parents separate or divorce, they face four major questions:

1. How can we best divide our property and move on with our separate lives?

2. How do we generate enough money to support ourselves separately?

3. How do we parent our children, now that we reside in two separate homes?

4. How do we share our children's expenses and respond effectively to their needs?

The court system calls these four parts: **Property Division, Spousal Support, Child Custody,** and **Child Support.** They are the major issues to be dealt with in all divorces with children. All four issues are extremely challenging to resolve when they are framed as a contest between two people. These four questions can be successfully answered when parents *negotiate a plan,* rather than fighting with each other in court in order to win. Negotiating a plan for their separate futures requires mutual effort. In helping parents to think mutually, we ask parents in mediation to consider negotiating from the following point of view: "You can only get a good, fair and just result for yourself when you also help obtain a good, fair and just result for the other parent."

In order to create a successful and fair child support plan, the questions of property division, spousal support, and the plan for sharing of parenting must also be answered by the parents in such a way that each parent can separately:

1) provide an adequate residence that accommodates their children;

2) have money left over to pay for each parent's personal living expenses;

3) have a cooperative co-parenting relationship with the other; and

4) have sufficient money to be able to provide for the physical, social, and emotional needs of their children, which include food, clothing, education costs, enrichment activities, and all the other items that parents agree are necessary for their children to grow and develop in a healthy way.

Essentially, mutual thinking is mutual planning. Such an approach allows both parents to place property, support and parenting into an integrated plan for the future that attempts to meet as many needs of the parents and their children as possible.

1. Mutual Thinking About Property Division

Mutual thinking can be achieved by realizing that, instead of fighting over who gets the house, the parents should work together to figure out how *both* can have adequate residences. In the court system, very little mutual thinking occurs. An attorney who represents a client in court and who is in battle mode with the opposing client and attorney over who will be awarded the home is required to argue that his or her client was a better parent and, therefore should be awarded custody of their children. Such an approach is necessary within the "System," because whoever wins custody usually gets the home, since judges usually award the home to the primary parent. Another contest strategy is to argue that one's client has the better ability to maintain the home or has better capacity to pay for the home, so that the children will be able to retain their established lifestyle.

In contrast to such separate thinking, mutual thinking changes the game from who gets the one house to how they mutually can create a plan for funding two separate residences for their children. This mutual planning approach creates a situation where the parents approach the problem of how to pay for two residences, rather than attacking each other over who wins the home and who, as the attorney will argue, "...must vacate the premises forthwith, taking only their necessary personal belongings."

2. Mutual Thinking About Parenting

Creating a parenting plan requires mutual thinking. In contrast, preparing for a custody trial requires contest thinking, using one's efforts and skills to show that the other parent is less fit. Just as there is no need to fight over the house, there is no need to fight over the children. This is accomplished when parents think mutually, discuss, and agree upon schedules of exchanges, transportation, expectations, communication protocols, and a host of other details as to how they will separately raise their children from two separate residences.

3. Mutual Thinking About Child Support

Parents begin with identifying the expenses of their children and creating a budget, which creates a mutual effort to discuss how they will share the costs of raising their children and actually reinforces the benefits of a mutual approach. In using the Child Support Account, parents also will find it necessary to address the changing needs of their children. Proponents of a contest approach believe that it is best to limit post-divorce contact and discussions between the parents, due to the fear that frequent discussions will simply generate more conflict. In contrast, the Child Support Account approach encourages necessary dialogue, which actually reinforces mutual thinking.

4. Mutual Thinking About Spousal Support (Alimony)

Spousal Support must be addressed in all cases, because the documents of divorce submitted to the court must address whether or not there will be any payment of spousal support from the higher income spouse to the lower income spouse and, if there is spousal support, for how long it will continue. This question can be resolved by asking mutual questions instead of trying to predict what the judge assigned to your case will rule. Here are the questions we ask both parents when one of them earns significantly less than the other parent:

a) Do you both agree that one of you is dependent upon the other for financial assistance, in order to meet your personal living expenses?

b) Do you both agree that a goal of these discussions in mediation is to try to reduce or eventually eliminate the financial dependency one of you has on the other, by creating a plan to increase earnings from employment, from property division, or from other income-producing assets of the lower- incomed parent?

c) What **plan** can the two of you agree upon that will end or reduce the financial dependency, and increase the level of self-sufficiency of the spouse who has been dependent on the other during the marriage?

It is easier to achieve mutual financial self-sufficiency after the divorce by framing all questions in a mutual manner and seeking a plan, rather than stirring up a contest that seeks a victory.

Change the Game by Asking Different Questions

When parents think mutually, rather than thinking only of their respective self-interests, there is a better chance for both to achieve fair results. Parents can more easily think mutually by asking different questions.

Existing child support systems calculate child support by using a "Formula" that can be computed by using a state-produced worksheet or a court-produced "Calculator." The formulas and tools used to compute the child support numbers are different for each state and are available to attorneys and to the general public. The calculations are referred to as "Guidelines," which means that the Court will run the essential information about both parents through the calculator. It will produce the Child Support Guidelines amount that the court then orders to be paid to the custodial (the "more time") parent. The information needed in this calculation in most states includes such items as each parent's income, health insurance costs, daycare costs, **and the time each parent spends with the children.** It is this last item over which parents usually fight hardest–the fight for the desired custody status, (i.e. for *more* time with the children), since that determines how much child support one will pay or receive.

All state child support formulas require parents to decide (or have the court decide for them) who is the "less-time parent," in order to complete the calculations. This requires courts and parents to ask the question, **"Who gets custody?"** Then, depending on the answer, one can proceed to calculate the amount to be paid by the "less-time" parent to the "more-time" (custodial) parent.

So, because the child support system is driven by this one important determination, when filing their petition for divorce, all parents must step into that court system and are forced to answer this divisive question: **Who is Going to Get the Children?**

When you enter the court system and are represented by an attorney, the overriding goal is to be AWARDED the WINNING custody label because then you will get the best child support outcome possible. An additional benefit of being awarded the winning custody label is that you avoid being designated as a "non-custodial, visiting parent," potentially until your youngest child turns 18 years old. Even though a lengthy and expensive contested custody trial can be, and usually is, avoided through negotiations, the settlement discussions are typically compromised by the pressing need to wind up with the "winning" custody label that gets the parent more time with the children. Then, upon custody being determined, the court can order child support and can order collections to begin, using wage-withholding against the "loser," so that money is sent to the "primary custodial" winner, *to use in whatever way that parent chooses to use it.*

Not only is asking about custody the wrong starting question in order to calculate meaningful child support, *it fails to address the main question of whether or not the child support amount actually meets the needs of the children.* It also avoids the crucial question of whether there is enough money remaining for each parent after support is calculated. In reality, the Guidelines serve as no more than a standardized formula applied to everyone in a way that cannot possibly create uniform fairness for every family. Such a simplistic formula cannot possibly consider all the individual differences in the costs of housing, debts, enrichment for their children, and all the other costs that may differentially affect each parent's budget after divorce.

By relying on the custody question as the starting point for determining child support, the court creates a competitive environment that discourages cooperation and makes it difficult for parents to work together. Common sense tells us that a bitter contest over who gets control of the children, and the money, will almost always generate future conflict between parents. However, cooperative negotiations will almost always result in a more constructive co-parenting relationship after divorce. **The Child Support Account solves this problem, in one of the most powerful ways possible**–it does so by asking different questions– ones that encourage parents to cooperate and communicate with each other about children and money. Most importantly, this new approach recognizes that most parents **desire** the cooperation of the other parent and that most parents are quite **capable** of cooperating, when supported in those efforts.

The Child Support Account creates cooperation by asking a future-focused question that requires a mutual effort to answer. This question is:

How will we share the costs of raising our children, given that we earn unequal incomes, spend different amounts of time with our children, and spend different amounts of money on them when they are with each of us?

This new question makes it less compelling to focus on who was the better parent (or worse parent) in the past, in order to position oneself to get more child support, or to resist demands to pay more child support. In the family mediation profession it is often said that the person who defines the problem has a great deal of power over how the problem is solved. By resisting the court's need to first define the problem as a "custody" problem and then rigidly apply the Guidelines formula, parents are able to focus on the *real* problem of how to properly construct a plan to share the costs of raising their children in the future.

It is more constructive to think of child support not as a legal problem, but as several separate parts of the entire task of raising children separately. In thinking about child support in a common sense way, we can view it as a combination of the following areas of mutually solvable problems:

- **A Housing problem:** Can we agree that we both have a need for adequate housing for our children?
- **A Budgeting and Bill-Paying problem:** Can we agree to consider what we can afford to spend on our children, as they approach their teen years when they will have more expenses?
- **An Income Problem:** Can we agree to try to increase our separate incomes, now that we must support two residences rather than one?
- **A Health Insurance problem:** Can we agree that if one of us is able to cover our children's health insurance at a lower cost, then we will, on our own, agree about adjusting our budget without having to go back to court for a costly, adversarial modification hearing?
- **A Parenting problem:** Can we agree that either of us can go out and buy a pair of shoes for our children without telling our children things like, "Go get the money from your Father/Mother"?
- **A Communication problem:** Can we learn how to effectively discuss our children's expenses and make shared decisions about what we can afford and what we cannot?

- **A Personal Boundary problem:** Can we support and respect each other's choices when, for example, one of us cannot afford to share in some discretionary expense for our children?

- **A Transition problem**: Can we agree to not argue about money issues in front of our children when we exchange them?

- **An Emotional problem:** Can we promise to keep our children out of the middle, even if we still have unresolved money issues left over from the marriage?

- **A Shared parenting problem:** Can we try to communicate better, because there are things that happen at each of our homes concerning our children that we must talk about?

- **A Future Financial Planning problem:** Can we agree to negotiate a way to have enough money for our children, to help them with college or other forms of higher education?

Here is what happens when "child support" becomes a "legal" problem, rather than a common sense plan to mutually craft: If you Google the question, "Why must child support be approved by the courts?", you first are directed to a full array of lawyer ads. The wording in these ads all play on your fears, and look something like these:

- Divorce can be ***complicated***...Let us help you ***protect*** your assets and your interests;

- We help you establish your custody ***rights;***

- We will be ***strong advocates*** for you in court;

- Read testimonials from our clients who ***prevailed*** in court;

- Don't let the other side ***get the best of you;***

- We will find ***hidden assets.***

The people who paid for those ads want you to be scared. ***Do not allow your fears to overtake you.*** That is how they get you hooked into the "contest- mentality" of the court system. That is how they turn common sense problems into "legal" issues. They are only correct about the fact that you should be extremely scared of your lack of knowledge about the law and scared of the possibility that you will fall into the abyss of the dysfunctional, adversarial legal system. This system is actually a high-stakes contest in which each of you is presumed to be incapable of figuring out what you need. The first step required in this adversarial system is for each of you to pay about $5,000 to $15,000 as a retainer, just to *start* a series of court proceedings that may or may not settle your contest, and with unknowable outcomes.

In reality, you do not need lawyers, or the legal system, to successfully create and use your Child Support Account. This common-sense approach is a better method for determining and managing child support and one that encourages cooperation and fairness for both of you.

The power of the Child Support Account is in its simplicity and common sense basis. To engage in this better way:

1) Invite your co-parent to build a parenting plan with you that allows each of you to have a meaningful and significant relationship with your children– one that is designed and guided by the two of you, not by the state.

2) Expect that you will need to talk with each other, negotiate, and make joint decisions about what you can afford to provide for your children and then work to accomplish the task of designing your Child Support Account.

3) Find a professional family mediator who can assist you with these tasks.[19]

Change the Game by Using Different Terms

Professional family mediators have come to understand that certain words and labels can have a destructive or a constructive effect on parenting relationships after separation and divorce. Using terms like "Parenting Plan" is much more helpful than using words like "Custody," which is a word that is most often used in connection with prisoners. "Visitation" is also used in reference to family contacts with prisoners, as well as in reference to funerals and hospitals. A new vocabulary is necessary in the search for less conflictual and more cooperative post-separation relationships. This is true for the language used in developing a time-sharing plan for your children, as well as the language used in negotiating how to share the costs of raising your children.

There are significant differences between terms used by courts and terms used by professional family mediators, who attempt to promote more productive negotiations. The court system uses "contest terminology" to describe the people who use the court. Consumers of the court process leave the court being labeled as either custodial parent, or non-custodial, visiting parent, and as payors of child support, or receivers of child support. A host of other labels has been created by the court to describe the various gradations of winners and losers in that system.

One of the lessons we have learned when assisting parents who choose to use the Child Support Account is that a constructive negotiating process results when more affirming terms are used to describe both the process and the people. The comparison below shows the differences between words applied by courts and words used in a constructive mediation process.

WORDS USED IN COURT / WORDS USED IN MEDIATION

WORDS USED IN COURT	WORDS USED IN MEDIATION
Visitation Schedule	Time-Sharing or Parenting Schedule
My Rights to Custody	Our Obligations to Our Children
Custody Determination	Developing a Parenting Plan
Ordering a Visitation Schedule	Mediating a Parenting Schedule
Child Custody Study/Evaluation	Seeking Advice of a Neutral Child Therapist Expert in Divorce
Calculating Guidelines Support	Creating a Budget for the Children
Shared Custody	Co-Parenting
Joint Custody	Co-Parenting
Legal Custody	Co-Parenting
Physical Custody	Co-Parenting
Primary Custody	Co-Parenting
Split Custody	Co-Parenting

COURT'S TERMS FOR PARENTS	MEDIATOR'S TERMS FOR PARENTS
Non-Custodial Visitor	Less-Time Parent
Custodial Parent	More-Time Parent
Deadbeat Dad	Dad
Absent Parent	Parent
Single Mom	Mom
Single Dad	Dad
Non-Psychological Parent	Parent
Primary Parent	Parent
Residential Parent	Parent
Non-Residential Parent	Less-time Parent
Non-Primary Parent	Less-time Parent

When developing your plan by using this book to create your own Child Support Account, avoid contest terms. Where possible, use the constructive terms from the right-hand column above when discussing matters related to co-parenting and the Child Support Account. In your negotiations with the other parent, using terms from the right-hand columns will make the discussions more productive.

By eliminating the contest, through mutually developing a parenting plan, it will be easier for you both to complete the joint work required to successfully use the Child Support Account. Realize that you have the power to change the game by:

- Thinking mutually;
- Asking different kinds of questions;
- Turning legal issues into common sense problems to solve;
- Using different words and terms from those that generate conflict;

You are now ready to learn the nuts and bolts of creating and using the Child Support Account.

Chapter Three:

How to Use the Child Support Account

Just as you would not start out to build a home without a blueprint, you need a road map and a guide to construct a child support plan. We have successfully used the following plan with parents who have utilized our assistance as professional family mediators:

STEP ONE: Ideally, both parents meet in consultation with a professional family mediator. This is a meeting with parents together, at the same time and in the same room, to learn about mediation and options, that include the Child Support Account, and to determine if the parents wish to proceed with mediation.

Parents may also construct agreements, using the Child Support Account on their own, without the use of a mediator. They first agree with each other to cooperate and avoid the financial and emotional costs of court, by negotiating a written child support plan that is submitted to court for approval, together with the other documents that satisfy state requirements for divorce, or for just determining child support, if not married. As noted above, in order to divorce you need court approval of your agreements. If you are never-married parents and do not have conflict about child support and parenting, you do not need to involve the court unless one of you is receiving state or federal welfare assistance. Using this book, along with other self-help divorce books and the Help-Aids on state court website pages, most parents are able to successfully create child support agreements. If needed, they can get help from divorce professionals, such as professional family mediators, financial consultants, and advisory attorneys. Many local court systems have set up self-help centers at the courthouse to assist people who file their documents of divorce without hiring a lawyer.

STEP TWO: In a mediation session or other cooperative setting, Dad and Mom are each asked to estimate the average monthly expenses of their children (See pg. 35, table 2-1) in several categories, adding others, as needed, and taking into account the ages of their children and the number of activities in which their children participate. The amounts listed are estimates, and parents do their best to predict future costs, based upon their past experiences. If a professional family mediator is not employed, the parents should make sure to sit down together to decide the expenses in each category for the next 12 months and then average each expense on a monthly basis, since child support is usually computed in monthly amounts.

The expenses listed in the "SHARED" (middle) column of Table 2-1 are the expenses of their children that parents agree to share and pay from the Account. The left and right "Paid Separately by Dad" and "Paid Separately by Mom" columns are not shared, but, instead, paid by each parent from their own separate funds.

"SEPARATE" expenses are shown in the budget, for three reasons: **1)** to remind both parents that paid-separately items may not be taken from the middle, shared column; **2)** to create boundaries that make using the Account clear, without requiring constant negotiations around discretionary items; and **3)** to give parents a sense of their children's total expenses when, for example, they are eating out, going on vacations, or other paid-separately items that are added to each parent's overall budget. It is very important to list these separate items that the parents agree are not to be paid from the shared column, because the quickest way to generate conflict when using the Account is to use money that is designated for specific expenses in the shared column for an "unauthorized" expense.

A sample list of expenses for a family with two children might look something like **Table 2-1** on the next page:

Table 2-1. Children's Monthly Expenses

Expense Item	Paid Separately by Dad	Shared	Paid Separately by Mom
Food and groceries	250		250
Eating out	150		150
Lunches at School		85	
Clothing		110	
Cell Phones		60	
Medical Insurance for the two children [If deducted from a paycheck, show who pays]	Deducted from Dad's paycheck	234	
Uncovered medical		34	
Uncovered dental		5	
Uncovered medication prescriptions		20	
Orthodontia		0	
Eyeglasses/Contact Lenses		35	
Car Insurance - daughter		110	
Dance (Costumes/Competition Costs)		250	
School Supplies & Backpacks		20	
Tutoring		127	
Sports (Soccer equipment, fees, and camp)		69	
Haircuts/ Hair Care		40	
Personal care items (cosmetics/other drugstore items)		45	
Gifts for friends' birthday parties		12	
TOTAL Expenses Anticipated to be Paid Separately by Each Parent: [Paid from their own separate funds]	400		400
TOTAL Shared Expenses for their children: [Items with a zero are also considered shared]		1,256	
Shared Costs Paid by Each [63%-37%]: [For example, if Dad earns $65k annual income and Mom earns $39k annual income, Dad's 63% of $1,256 is $791, and Mom's 37% of $1,256 is $465	791		465
Medical Insurance Paid Directly by Dad: [This is reimbursed to Dad, by subtracting it from his 63%, because he pays it directly through paychecks, and it is included in his contribution to the shared column]	-234		
Monthly Amount Deposited into Account by Each:	557		465

The important task here is for parents to **talk face-to-face about what it might cost to raise their children separately in the future.** These budgets are usually estimates, since this is not an exact science, but a method for eliciting cooperative and useful planning. See Chapter Four, which gives the details for creating a Budget.

STEP THREE: Parents determine what they each will contribute to the shared budget, based on their respective earnings. Parents earning equal annual incomes will contribute equally to the shared, middle column total. Parents earning unequal incomes will usually pay unequally to the Account, with the higher income parent contributing more. The framework is easy to use. The amount that each parent contributes is a percentage of the shared column total. This proportional approach is based upon the common-sense principle that the higher-income parent will pay more towards children's shared expenses than will the lower-income parent.

Here is an example, using the incomes of both parents, as detailed above: If Dad's income is $65,000 per year and Mom's income is $39,000 per year.

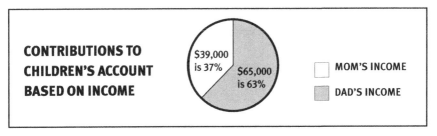

TOTAL COMBINED INCOME: $39,000 + $65,000 = $104,000

Mom's Income of $39,000 = 37% (Mom's pro rata percentage)
Total combined income of $104,000

Dad's Income of $65,000 = 63% (Dad's pro rata percentage)
Total combined income of $104,000

Using the above income example, Father's income of $65,000 represents 63% of their total combined income of $104,000, and Mother's income of $39,000 represents 37% of their combined incomes. In the above budget, the total shared expenses for two children are $1,256 each month. Father would deposit $557 per month into the Child Support Account. In addition, he would have $234 credited for the children's health insurance costs as a payroll deduction at work, for a total contribution of $791 per month, while Mother would deposit $465 per month.[20]

Once the contributions to the Account are agreed upon, each parent may spend from the Child Support Account to purchase any of the "shared" items for their children. Both parents must agree to spend only within the budgeted amounts. As explained above, expenses such as recreation, entertainment, and eating out with their children are not paid through the joint account, because they agree that those expenses are considered to be the personal expenses of each parent. Only expenses that are agreed upon as "shared" are paid from the joint account. Interestingly, many parents have told us that having a budget of targeted expenses helps them become more frugal in their joint efforts to stay within the budget. This method is not unlike any business enterprise trying to budget for next year's expenses, and then attempting to keep within those expense projections during the coming year.

In actual practice, many parents have developed purchasing patterns during the marriage that continue after divorce, such as Dad paying for the car expenses, and Mom purchasing the clothes for their children. Some couples may have used a special "household account" during the marriage that can be converted to the Child Support Account and used only for children's shared expenses after the separation or divorce.

STEP FOUR: Parents decide when and how often they will revisit the budget, as well as re-calculate their pro-rata contributions. We suggest that parents review the expense history at least after the passage of twelve months, to see how close actual expenditure totals matched their initial projections. Many parents have used the budget as a way to explain to their children that there will be limits on what can be spent for clothing and other items. This has even resulted in children urging their parents to revisit the budget and increase the line-item amount for clothing.

In contrast, rather than encouraging, or even allowing, frequent court hearings to review the court-ordered child support amounts, courts deliberately make it difficult to modify child support. Moreover, a parent seeking to increase or decrease their child support amount most often must show a "substantial change of circumstances." Courts operate on the doctrine of "finality," which may be a good idea for business disputes, where once a lawsuit for damages has been determined, it needs to be put to rest without endless litigation. However, children's needs are constantly changing, and in today's world of self-employed contract workers, parental incomes frequently change, as well. And, a child turning 16 and getting a driver's license will generate new expenses, e.g. car insurance and fuel, which can add several hundred dollars a month to the children's budget.

So, it is a good idea to sit down with the other parent at least yearly. Some parents choose the end of April each year, after taxes have been filed. Parents can then disclose any changes in their respective incomes and adjust their proportional contributions to the Child Support Account.

Of course, it is not practical, or even possible, to be accurate to the penny with the projections of expenses, or parental contributions to the Account since, for example, there may be a sport that a child is no longer playing mid-year, or parental incomes might change during the year. Yet, the Child Support Account is a significantly better approach. It certainly is better than receiving a terse email from the other parent saying: "This will inform you that $850 per month is what your attorney and the court ordered me to send to you, and since you continue to fight me on custody, you can pay for their car insurance!"

The sample language in Chapter 5 converts the above ideas into language that can be submitted to the court and followed by parents who choose to use the Child Support Account.

Chapter Four:
Creating a Budget of Shared Expenses of the Children

When using the Child Support Account, it is essential to include a budget of the children's expenses, as part of the agreement. The first task is to cooperatively negotiate, either during or outside of mediation, which items will be shared children's expenses and which will be expenses that are each parent's separate responsibility. The second task is to determine and agree upon estimated monthly amounts for each budget item. The children's expenses that will be shared are the average monthly recurring costs of raising children. Most parents have a rough idea of these costs, because usually one or both have been paying these for some time during the marriage. Parents also can decide which expenses to designate as separate, such as eating out, recreation, entertainment, and vacations. Also, parents may decide to designate *anything* as a shared expense, which is just fine, provided they both agree.

Decisions about whether to place an item in the "shared" column, or in the "separate" columns, and determining whether a given expense is "extraordinary," are really based on common sense and agreement between the parents. Our guide, below, takes into account the combined wisdom of thousands of parents in our practices whom we have asked, "Do you think this should be a shared item, or should it be paid separately by each of you, as your own expense?"

REALITY CHECK: Most parents (and adults, in general) do not regularly operate on a budget. However, parents raising children in two separate residences will have to figure out how to pay for their children's expenses. They first must agree on the shared expenses and what can be afforded, given each parent's particular financial circumstances. Creating a budget together actually reduces the likelihood of future conflict about supporting their children. A budget is also important because most parents do not have unlimited funds.

As parents create a budget of their children's expenses, they should ask these critical questions regarding every **shared** expense:

1) What is the average monthly cost for each item? and,

2) Is the item necessary and affordable?

These questions help to keep the discussion within a practical, rather than emotional, framework and as a rational, constructive, problem-solving process.

Categories of Children's Expenses

Some common categories of children's expenses are listed below, but you may wish to add or delete categories to fit your own special circumstances. Maybe your children need tutoring, or you decide to include the cost of a family pet, both of which may be placed in the shared category column. The final budget should reflect your own agreements as to relevant categories and your estimates of costs. One of the best aspects of the Child Support Account is that the bank statements for the Account automatically provide a monthly record of all the expenses of the children, and the amounts paid, within the Account.

One of the benefits of creating and using the Child Support Account is that parents have the opportunity to decide for themselves whether to put an expense item into the shared column, or exclude it from the Child Support Account, by paying separately for the item from their own personal funds. From our observations of parents discussing this issue, some of the most common questions are:

- "Is the expense a usual and necessary cost of raising our children?"
- "Can this particular expense routinely be estimated or predicted?"
- "Is this an expense that is similar to the costs of taking the children out for ice cream–a situation in which you would not expect the other parent to have to pay for a portion of it?"
- (Asked of the mediator) "What have other parents done in this situation?"

HOW OFTEN ARE EXPENSES SHARED?

Whether an expense is *Seldom Shared, Usually Shared,* or *Never Shared* is based upon our observations in watching many couples negotiate this part of the Child Support Account.

FOOD: Seldom shared. No one wants to stand at the checkout counter and place the little plastic separator between their own food and their children's food. Food is usually considered a separate expense, paid for by each parent from his or her own separate funds. This simplifies the use of the Child Support Account, by eliminating disagreements about what is a proper purchase within the food budget (Consider the difficulty that the government has had in setting rules as to whether food stamps should be used for junk food, tobacco, lobster, or alcohol). For parents using the Child Support Account who have equal time-sharing with their children, and have similar incomes, it is assumed they have equivalent purchasing power. However, for parents who have unequal time-sharing with the kids, resulting in more food costs for one parent, there is still a way to use the Account and still manage the imbalance in food costs. In such a case, parents can agree on a dollar amount that the more-time parent may use each month from the shared Account for their additional food costs.

An example of this would be parents who wish to use the Child Support Account, but one of the parents is unable to engage in equivalent time sharing, because of temporarily working out of town, or not having enough room for the children in his or her current residence, or for some other reason. We have observed parents estimating some extra amount, when one of the parents is providing food for the children a majority of the time. Or, if for a majority of the time, the more-time parent is driving the children to sports and to other activities, he or she can also use the Account to reimburse the other parent for the extra cost of gas. The basic idea of the budget is that it should be tailored to the individual needs of each family. It is important to understand that there is no actual average family, and therefore, each family must arrange its own unique and most feasible budget possible.

To keep it simple, the less-time parent might add $300-$400 in monthly contribution to the Account to compensate for the amount that would have been spent on the children for food, had that parent been able to spend half the time with them. This allows the more-time parent to be reimbursed for the extra food expenses.

CHILDREN'S SCHOOL LUNCHES: *Usually shared.* Many parents pay school lunch accounts automatically from the Child Support Account to the schools. However, occasionally, parents will disagree about the cost, citing the fact that one parent takes the time to prepare bag lunches, thus saving money, while the other parent chooses to use the school lunch program. In this type of dispute, the resolution may be that the cost is not shared, and it becomes the sole expense of the parent who likes the convenience of the school lunch program and is willing to pay for it on the days that the children are with that parent.

EATING OUT: *Seldom shared.* Parents in mediation typically treat eating out as a discretionary expense, to be paid separately. It would generate a good deal of unnecessary conflict if one parent called the other and said: "You owe me $2.75 for the $5.50 I spent on our children for snacks last night between soccer games." Common sense suggests that this should be your own separate, discretionary expense.

CELL PHONES: *Usually shared.* While there is great controversy regarding children having their own cell phones, it has become a reality. For some parents, this is often considered a safety issue, so they can know if their child has arrived safely at the child's other residence or if there is an emergency. Parents disagreeing about whether their child needs a cell phone presents an opportunity for them to discuss and create agreed upon rules regarding their children's use of cell phones. Such rules can also become the basis for reaching agreement about sharing the costs of the cell phone. They can choose to have the costs paid separately by one parent, or agree upon some other resolution.

CLOTHING: *Usually shared.* Although some parents agree that they will each separately purchase clothing for their children and keep them at their separate homes (and not include clothes in the shared column), most children end up wearing most of their clothes at both homes, making it easier just to buy all the children's clothing from shared funds. More often, one of the parents takes responsibility for buying most of their children's clothing and uses the Child Support Account for doing so. If that was the case during the time they lived together, it might make sense to have that parent continue to buy the clothes. Some parents distinguish between clothing items paid from the Child Support Account and special clothing items, such as gifts, or items for special occasions, which the parents may pay for separately. A common complaint voiced by parents in high conflict is that one parent does not return clothes purchased by the other parent, resulting in conflict spilling over to their children. Parents who have been able to create an integrated, mutually fair settlement agreement, as described in Chapter Two, are usually able to phone or text the other parent and say: "Please send back some underwear and socks, because I am getting low on them. Let me know if we need to purchase more of them, using the Child Support Account. Do you know if we have enough money left in the clothing category of our budget for their September school clothes?"

The conflict over returning children's clothing purchased by the other parent is usually more about some other unresolved issue between the parents. In mediation, we attempt to drill down and help parents identify their underlying interests. Often, we find that it is really a communication problem, or perhaps a beginning failure to follow agreed upon commitments to pay attention to the small details of their plan that, over time, can become huge. Parents using the Child Support Account will, occasionally, experience difficulty in executing the plan, which helps them learn what they must do differently, in order to keep it on track.

MEDICAL AND DENTAL INSURANCE: *Always shared.* By statute in most states, this cost is always shared. One parent actually pays for it, since most of the time medical insurance for their children is set up by a plan through that parent's employer as a payroll deduction. As such, this is always in the "shared" column. You will need information about the cost of coverage that shows what portion of the premium cost is attributable only to the children's coverage. The person funding the health insurance is given a credit in the Account, as detailed in Chapter Three, in the sample language below and in Chapter Five.

UNCOVERED AND UNINSURED MEDICAL AND DENTAL COSTS: *Always shared.* Again, by statute in almost all states, all medically related costs not covered by insurance are also shared. Parents will attempt to estimate these costs, based on past experience and their special circumstances. Disputes are sometimes generated over medical and dental costs and the particular type of healthcare treatment needed, such as whether an out-of-network specialist needs to be retained. Yet, most parents are able to resolve these issues by agreeing to communicate with each other about unexpected medical and dental costs for their children. By paying them from the Child Support Account, parents eliminate the need to keep detailed records of who must be reimbursed if one fronted the cost, as is typically the case when using the Child Support Guidelines.

HAIR CUTS AND HAIR CARE: *Sometimes shared.* Especially for some teens, items in this category can become expensive. During negotiations, the parents can agree upon what they are willing to cover and what would exceed the amount they are willing to share.

PERSONAL CARE ITEMS: *Sometimes shared.* These items may include grooming products, cosmetics, personal care items, and other non-grocery items needed by their children. Generally, the discussions about items in this category do not produce controversy. Some parents find it a nominal expenditure and leave it out of the budget, or they may include it as part of each household's separate expenses and not passed through the joint account.

CHILDCARE: *Usually shared.* This category includes daycare costs, and before-school and after-school program costs, and also childcare costs for days off from school, and summer care. Child Support Guidelines in many states require these costs to be entered into the basic child support calculations and shared proportionally, based on gross or net incomes. In addition, discussions about payment of childcare expenses may benefit from consultation with a tax consultant who can advise on tax deductions and exemptions for families when filing separately. Conflict sometimes arises over whether the childcare is absolutely necessary. Usually, the test of whether it is discretionary or necessary is whether the daycare is needed to allow one or both parents to work. However, most parents agree that, when a parent who is scheduled to be with the children has an evening out without the children, costs of a babysitter are paid separately by the person incurring the cost.

EDUCATION EXPENSES: *Usually shared.* School field trips, school pictures, backpacks, books, school supplies, and other agreed-upon expenses are all in this category. There usually is very little controversy over these expenses. Sometimes, parents have conflict about whether they can afford the tuition of a private school for their child. Annually reviewing their children's budget usually resolves these types of issues.

EXTRA-CURRICULAR, ENRICHMENT ACTIVITIES, AND CAMPS: *Usually shared.* This category of expenses can sometimes create conflict. All parents would like to give their children as much of these kinds of opportunities as they can. However, the discussion often centers on what they can actually afford. If parents decide they cannot afford an activity, both parents will then share the task of informing their children.

SPORTS FEES AND SPORTS EQUIPMENT: *Usually shared.* For some families, this can be a huge expense. Often, both parents agree in advance and have an interest in seeing their children play sports. If only one parent is avid about it, they can agree that their child may participate in the sport, but the avid parent will, separately, pay all expenses associated with the sport and, perhaps, also provide transportation. Sometimes, both parents agree to keep funding the sport after considering their child's commitment and enjoyment. This item often requires in-depth discussions in mediation.

Sometimes a child may begin with one sport, lose interest, and want to switch to a different activity. When this situation arises, parents need to discuss it and make a decision about whether or not this should occur. This presents several opportunities for parents to have important discussions with each other and with their children about:

1) What is a fair process for evaluating the child's request?

    a) What is the child's reason for changing?

    b) What is the status of previously paid fees?

    c) What are the fees for the new activity or sport and equipment?

    d) What are the parents' values about keeping commitments?

2) What will be the impact on the child?

3) What will be the impact on the children's budget?

4) Can the parents agree upon what they will do if this problem reoccurs?

When parents have exhausted their discussions on this issue, what is their next course of action? How will they tell the child about their decision?

We have observed that, if parents work together on this problem and arrive at a mutual decision that is jointly communicated to the child, the willingness of all to engage in this discussion will have a positive impact on the child, as well as on strengthening the parents' commitment to the principles of the Child Support Account.

AUTOMOBILE EXPENSES: *Usually shared.* For those families with a child of driving age and if there is a car available to use, some or all the costs, including driver's education, insurance, car maintenance and repair, gas, and license fees, can be listed in the budget as shared. However, some parents may also agree that, if their child is employed, then that child will share in paying some of these expenses.

GIFTS: *Sometimes shared.* A child's gifts to others, like to a friend at a birthday party, are usually shared, using the Child Support Account. However, gifts from a parent to a child are usually not shared, since these are seen as discretionary, and paid separately by each parent. A discussion is usually required to decide how gifts from their children to each parent (and grandparents) for birthdays, Mother's Day, Father's Day, and holidays will be funded.

RECREATION AND ENTERTAINMENT: *Almost never shared.* This category is almost never shared. Parents usually decide that it is best to keep this category as part of each parent's discretionary spending, because it is too difficult to monitor. If it were shared, a parent might feel obligated to check with the other parent every time that parent chose any type of entertainment activity, and it would be too intrusive. However, parents may decide to share some of these unanticipated expenses, on a case-by-case basis. For example, a parent may need to accompany a child who wishes to attend a concert where friends are performing. The parents would need to agree in advance whether to share the expense of admission.

VACATIONS AND TRAVEL: *Almost never shared.* This is similar to the recreation and entertainment expenses, and it is not considered part of their children's joint account. However, some parents may include travel expenses as a shared item if they have a long-distance parenting arrangement, because such travel expenses are seen as necessary to maintain parent-child relationships. Parents may also share expenses when a child travels as part of a school opportunity, a membership organization, or with a friend's family.

SAVINGS FOR POST-HIGH SCHOOL EDUCATION TUITION: *Shared, if parents are in agreement and able to contribute.* Parents who can afford to designate such savings as part of the shared Account may include this in the budget. Most states do not require it as a part of child support.

POST-HIGH SCHOOL EDUCATION LIVING EXPENSES: *Shared, if parents are able to contribute.* Some parents find the Child Support Account so useful for managing their children's living expenses that they continue to use the Account through the Post-High School Education, Trade School or College years, even though their divorce decree does not require such a continuation.

PET EXPENSES: *Sometimes shared.* Costs of food, boarding, and veterinary expenses for family pets have been included as shared expenses for their children, even if the pet is primarily at one home. The differences among families lead each to arrive at their own conclusions about this expense.

HOUSING: *Seldom shared.* Housing costs of each parent are not shared. If the goal of ending the relationship and living separately is to create physical, as well as financial boundaries, the parents will separately pay for their own respective housing. Rather than share housing costs, the more common solution is to have the higher-income parent pay spousal support to the lower-income parent, which could be used to equalize the housing expenses. In that way, there are conditions on the payment of spousal support, as well as an end point to the spousal support, in the great majority of cases. Many parents in mediation are willing to assist with housing costs in the form of spousal support, because they see that such support is ultimately helping their children.

On rare occasions, a shared housing cost relating to their children might consist of the parents paying the rent for their child who is attending college or other post-high school training programs. Or, in a small number of cases, when the parents are "bird-nesting,"[21] they will share the cost of their joint homestead, since their children reside there full-time. In a handful of cases, parents have also included the costs of rent or mortgage, utilities, and other costs of housing in the shared column, when needed, in order to subsidize one parent in obtaining adequate housing (e.g. for a larger apartment, in order to give siblings separate rooms) until such time as both parents are able to pay for their own separate housing costs. In mediation, special attention will be given to the option of obtaining adequate housing for both parents. This is accomplished by both parents creating a budget not only for their children, but also for their own living expenses. An important part of one's budget of expenses is the housing costs. Planning for adequate housing for each parent is one of the challenges of jointly parenting after divorce.

The success of the Child Support Account is largely due to parents' capacity to uniquely create an individual plan that works for their family. As illustrated above, most categories of children's expenses require discussion and agreement before completing a children's budget. For this reason, the success of the Account is also enhanced when using an experienced professional family mediator.

Using the Child Support Account changes the co-parenting relationship by changing the way the parents are linked. In a court setting, when one parent wins, the other parent loses. When using the Child Support Account, parents begin to see that the actions of one will actually increase the likelihood that the other's needs can also be met.

When parents spend time building a budget for themselves and for their children, they are more likely to become motivated to jointly solve the universal problem of not having enough money to run two households. Avoiding the contest model of court-ordered solutions can also result in mutual agreements that adopt a fairness principle that calls for equivalently sharing the burdens of divorce. In mediation, we have called this "equal belt-tightening."

Chapter Five:

Making your *Child Support Account* Acceptable to Your Court

Sample Language

The following sample language has been refined over many years of submitting to the court legal documents that successfully have become approved by the judge or child support hearing officer. These paragraphs can effectively be used in the courts of any state, and the paragraphs can serve as the template for building your own Child Support Account language. This sample language has proved especially useful when first introducing the Child Support Account to judges and child support hearing officers who might initially have an unfavorable attitude towards deviating from traditional child support Guidelines systems.

Finally, the sample language that we suggest you consider using in your court filings to obtain court approval will always look like this type-face you are reading now in this sentence.

You will be building your own Child Support Account language to fit your own fact situation. So that you can be ready to respond to questions from a judge who, in court, might ask you questions about the Account, here are the seven sections of sample language that we created for our clients to use in Minnesota courts, together with our comments to help you use the suggested language in your own court filings. In your own state, all seven sections will be needed in your filings. If your submitted document is not approved, the reason is usually that some piece is missing. More detail is better, until the Child Support Account concept becomes more firmly rooted in Family Law.

The sample language follows these seven steps:

1. Show what the Guidelines would require one of you to pay to the other, if you were to follow the State Child Support Guidelines. Be detailed in setting out for the court the numbers you would insert into the formula, in order to arrive at a final child support Guidelines amount that you would pay or would receive.

2. Summarize for the court how the Child Support Account works, and request approval.

3. Explain why you are deviating from state Guidelines, and list as many reasons as possible to justify the deviation.

4. Include a detailed budget for the expenses of your children which you will each be responsible for paying.

5. Describe how and when you will change your respective contributions to the Account as well as when you will change or add categories of children's expenses.

6. Promise to keep your spending within the budget projections.

7. Close with a statement that you will not call upon the court to step in and supervise your use of the Child Support Account, and agree that either of you may choose to stop using it at any time and for any reason. If it is no longer working for you, acknowledge that you will then be required to follow your state Guidelines (Use of the Account is entirely voluntary).

For your court filings, you can use the sample language as it is presented below. Be sure to insert your personal information for your particular state's child support Guidelines formula, including the income from each parent, the number of children, and other information required to calculate your state formula. The above seven steps have worked well for cases in Minnesota. If you live in a state that always approves *upward* deviations from the Guidelines (i.e., higher child support than required by the Guidelines), but not *downward* deviations (i.e., lower child support than required by the Guidelines), you might want to add the following statement:

By examining the budget totals contained herein, it is clear that our children are receiving more total support than would be received when compared to the Guidelines calculation.

By adding up all contributions to the children from both parents, one can often show to the court that more total support money will be provided to the children than would be provided by a routine calculation of Guidelines child support.

STEP ONE: SHOW WHAT THE GUIDELINES WOULD REQUIRE ONE OF YOU TO PAY TO THE OTHER

Start by determining what your state child support Guidelines formula would require you to pay, given your incomes, the number of children, and who has custody, or which parent spends more time with the children, and which parent spends less time with the children.

The actual language of Step One that you may use to insert into the documents submitted to court can look like this:

> **Amount of (Your State) Guidelines Support.** The parents have determined the **(Enter Your State)** Child Support Guidelines would require Mother to pay Father the approximate sum of $144 per month for child support, which is based upon the following:
>
> 1) Father earns $65,000 gross income per year ($5,417 gross per month); and Mother earns $39,000 gross income per year ($3,250 gross per month); and
>
> 2) Father and Mother are not exchanging spousal maintenance; and
>
> 3) Father pays for the children's health insurance premiums, in the amount of $234 per month, and the dental insurance premiums are included; and
>
> 4) Mother and Father have no daycare costs for the children; and,
>
> 5) Mother and Father are following an approximately equivalent timesharing parenting schedule.

HOW TO CALCULATE YOUR GUIDELINES CHILD SUPPORT AMOUNT AND INCLUDE IT WITH YOUR COURT FILING

All Child Support Accounts must start with the above, showing what you would pay in child support if you followed your state Guidelines. You must show first what you are deviating from in order to obtain approval by the court. This will also assure the court that you are making an informed decision. *More importantly though, once you are given approval to use the Child Support Account, you would also be opting out of Support and Collections forcibly taking money out of one parent's checking account and sending it to the receiver of child support unless you decided to terminate use of the Child Support Account; in such a case you could opt back in to using Support and Collections.* To find out what your state Guidelines would require for your particular situation, go to a website provided by your state court system.

You may find a state-issued website that allows you to fill in the number of children you have, each of your incomes, and other information it requires. It will then calculate the amount of child support required under their Guidelines.[22] This website will require you to show who has custody or who is the more-time parent, under your schedule. When trying to understand the Guidelines, specifically as it relates to time, do not be confused by terms such as shared custody, joint custody, dual custody, legal custody, physical custody, split custody or, if you live in Texas, the managing conservator and the possessory conservator. These labels are all versions of a concept of "ownership of the children," and you will not need them since you are deviating from the contest mode of the Guidelines. As we have stated repeatedly, all Guidelines calculations are driven by who has more time and who has less time with their children, and by who is the less-income parent. In those cases of equal time-sharing and unequal income, some state formulas call for a small amount of support to be sent from the higher income parent to the lower income parent. Try your best to muddle through the Guidelines calculation and even if the judge looks at your paperwork and finds that you miscalculated, the judge or the clerk at the self-help desk, hopefully, will assist you.

Your state may only provide you with a worksheet. If so, courts often have a self-help desk staffed with very accommodating people,[23] and they might provide you with child support calculation forms. You will need to compute exactly what the Guidelines would require one of you to pay to the other as child support, as if you were following the Guidelines formula. Then, you can insert the numbers in the sample language provided here to show the court that you are aware of the Guidelines' amount. For purposes of cooperative negotiations, you might find it easier to refer in the documents to both Mother and Father as simply "Parents," and if you need to include labels, you can refer to the "more-time parent" and the "less-time parent." If you find this task difficult, you may get help from a professional family mediator.

STEP TWO: PROVIDE A SUMMARY OF HOW THE ACCOUNT WORKS

Next, describe the mechanics of how the Child Support Account works, and request approval to deviate from the Guidelines.

> However, Father and Mother will not follow the Guidelines, and will respectfully request a deviation that allows both parents to more effectively support their child(ren). The parents have agreed to an arrangement for sharing the costs of raising their children that calls for itemizing all expenses related to their children, in the amount of $1,256 per month, and sharing these costs on a pro-rata basis according to their gross annual incomes. This amount will be calculated on the basis of determining the percentage of their respective gross annual incomes in relation to their combined gross annual income. Father's gross income is $65,000 per year, and Mother's gross income is $39,000 per year. Mother earns 37% of their combined total income and she agrees to pay $465 each month into the joint account; Father earns 63% of their combined total incomes and he agrees to pay $791 each month into the joint account. This $791 includes $234 of Health Insurance for the children deducted from Father's salary, and $557 cash paid into the Account by Father, for a total contribution of $791 each month.
>
> Therefore, each parent shall contribute towards the below-listed expenses of their children, set forth in the "shared" column below, by depositing these amounts monthly into a children's joint account. The itemized "shared" expenses below shall be paid by either parent from that Account.

Here, you are introducing the court to the core concept of the Child Support Account and are stating that you wish deviate from the Guidelines and instead use the Account. You are describing in this section how each parent will pay money each month into the joint bank account. The money that each of you pay will be proportional, according to your incomes. That is, the higher income parent will contribute more to the Account than will the lower income parent. This concept of the higher income parent contributing more to the cost of raising their children is a fairness principle that is basic to all state Guidelines formulas, and, if you are not contributing proportionally to the Account, you should be prepared to explain your rationale in case your judge or hearing officer questions your departure from the norm.

We have had instances in which the court has allowed equal, rather than proportional contributions to the Account, even when parents' incomes are substantially unequal, because both parents have the ability to earn equivalent incomes if they choose, but one of them has made a voluntary choice to work part-time. In such cases, we will include language that states that, while the lower income parent has the potential to earn more, that parent has made a voluntary choice to earn less than the other parent. Or, we have inserted language that asserts that the lower income parent is in possession of significant non-marital (in California, this is called "non-community") assets, and is quite able to share equally in the costs of raising their children, even though their incomes may be unequal. In reality, the court simply wants to know that, if you deviate from the norm by rejecting the Guidelines, and also by rejecting the fairness principle of proportional sharing of children's costs, you have done so knowingly, and are aware of the other choices you could have made (Judges do not want cases coming back to be reopened, with someone saying: "Your Honor, I didn't really understand the ramifications of what I was doing."). Another response to a judge questioning you in detail about your fairness choices is to point out that you have included an escape hatch (set forth in Step Seven) which allows either one of you to terminate the use of the Account at any time, and for any reason, and to revert back to following the Guidelines formula that is in effect in your state at the time you terminate using the Child Support Account.

For the majority of parents, who will likely follow proportional contributions to the Account, you need to be specific setting forth the actual pro-rata result of your income differences, so that the court can see the dollar amount you will each contribute to the Account. In the Minnesota sample language case (in this chapter above), Father will be contributing $791 per month to the Account, and Mother will be contributing $465 each month to the Account, because Father's income is greater than Mother's, and they are following equivalent time-sharing of their children.

Finally, in the last paragraph of the above section, you are introducing the court to the concept of the "shared column" of expenses and the "separate columns" of expenses. As you will see in more detail in the budget grid that follows, you will be including a detailed budget of your children's expenses. Most of your children's expenses will be placed in the shared column and will be paid from the Account. However, some of your children's discretionary expenses will be paid by each of you, as your own expense, and are listed as "paid separately" by only one parent, so that the court, as well as the two parents, understand what expenses are not permitted to be paid through the shared Child Support Account.

STEP THREE: EXPLAIN WHY THE DEVIATION FROM GUIDELINES IS IN THE BEST INTERESTS OF YOUR CHILDREN

Explain why you are deviating from the Guidelines, and list as many reasons as possible for the deviation. Paragraphs **a)** through **f)** summarize why the Child Support Account method benefits your children, and is in their best interests:

> The parents prefer to use this method of sharing the costs of raising their children, instead of one parent sending a sum of money to the other, because this sharing of children's costs:
>
> **(a)** Permits both parents to pay for items that their children need when their children are with that parent, instead of telling their children they must ask the recipient of child support to always purchase necessary items for them; and

This language (in Paragraph a) tells the court that you are not constantly in conflict, and you do not need to designate one of you as the custodial parent to make important financial decisions *[Remember the chapter describing flawed- thinking? The adversarial system has an assumption that you cannot cooperate]*. You are saying to the court: "We can cooperate, and both of us wish to purchase items for our children. It makes sense for both of us to use a common source of money to pay for our children's expenses. After all, that is what we did during our marriage, and there is no reason to change now. Besides, it would be quite cumbersome to tell our children that they must always get the money from the other parent, since both of us are still their parents."

> **(b)** Provides a record of expenses incurred by their children, or on their behalf, thereby allowing the parents to more easily make future modifications of the child support as their children's expenses change in the future; and

This language (in paragraph b) supports your request to deviate and says you want to create a record of what you spend, for reference to use in future meetings where you expect to adjust the budget to reflect new and changing expense needs for your children (The administrators at the Court House would be fired if they said, "We don't need to keep a record of what we spend, we will just continue to use the same budget we used when we built the Court House in 1902"). Paragraph (b) also addresses the false assumption about what is covered by "basic support," and that you plan to keep a record of it as it is spent (by keeping bank or credit card records), because you also anticipate that you may be making modifications of the child support as your children's expenses change over time.

> **(c)** Does not tie child support to time with their children, thereby separating the parenting time discussions from its effect on the amount of child support exchanged; and

Paragraph (c) tells the court that you do not wish to trade days for dollars, and that you find it easier to reach agreements about child support when time with the children does not control the amount of money that must be used for your children. Moreover, it indicates that you refuse to get into a custody battle just to get enough money to pay your bills. In the mediation process that we have developed, parents are also asked to create a personal expense budget for themselves, so it is possible to ensure that both Mom and Dad also have enough money for their basic needs. It is difficult to parent children when one cannot pay the rent or mortgage. If there is not enough money to pay for reasonable costs of both parents and their children, then there needs to be a discussion about increasing incomes, reducing costs, or temporarily borrowing from assets to reduce expenses (It is always wise to remember that only the federal government can do deficit financing forever).

(d) Allows for periodic adjustments to child support, by modifying the amount deposited into the Account from each parent upon review of changes to each parent's income;

Paragraph (d) assures the court that, in addition to adjustments for changes in children's expenses, you have also anticipated that you will likely need to change your respective contributions to the Account if your incomes change substantially. Here, you are telling the court that you have included a method to modify each of your contributions to the Account, on your own. You will not be bringing endless motions in court to modify the Guidelines child support each time one of the parent's income changes.

(e) Is a continuation of the joint consultation and decision-making that naturally takes place between the parents during their marriage (and/or during their separation);

Paragraph (e) tells the court that you are candidates for using this type of child support arrangement because, basically, you are cooperative parents.

(f) Is consistent with the parents' choice to mediate their divorce, which is evidenced by their shared parenting plan that requires them to share (proportionally or equally) in the future costs of raising their children.

In paragraph (f) you are letting the court know you have completed a parenting plan and have already had preliminary discussions about equal sharing, or proportional sharing of your children's expenses.

Finally, you can close with a statement about how the children's best interests are served and then proceed to a display of the actual budget Table 5-1 of children's expenses:

The parents believe it is in their children's best interests to reserve the issue of one parent paying child support to the other, and, instead, to require the sharing of expenses as provided herein.

There are no arrearages in child support[25], as of the

date of the final hearing. The parents intend to use a joint account to manage and disburse the funds necessary for payment of the "shared" children's costs. Separate expenses to be paid by each parent directly and not from the joint account are also set forth below. The following represents an "initial budget of expenses," and the parents expect that, from time to time, they will meet and review or adjust these expense estimates.

These last two paragraphs are transitional. By indicating that you are "reserving the issue of one parent paying child support to the other," you are letting the court know that you will never abandon your children and will always support them, either through the Child Support Account, or by reverting back to the Guidelines. [26] You also introduce the court to the budget, which is next. Notice that you will be calling it an "initial budget of expenses," because you expect that the budget will be adjusted, from time to time in the future.

Before moving to a discussion about budgets, it is important to say one last word about the concept of "deviating from the Guidelines." If the court prohibits you from deviating from the Guidelines and adopting the Child Support Account, you can still use the Account, after first passing the money through support and collections, but it is much less cumbersome to obtain approval to deviate in the first place. We expect that, as more courts become familiar with how the Child Support Account works, there will be less resistance to approve deviations from Guidelines.

Do not say that *you will not send child support,* but rather indicate in your documents that you are choosing to support your children in a different manner. You are telling the court that you do not wish to have one of you send child support money to the other, but rather that you will both support your children, by sending support money directly to the Child Support Account, which, in turn, is used to support your children.

The reasons you have listed for deviating from Guidelines will focus on how children are kept out of the middle by parents using the Child Support Account, and how it is in children's best interests to use the Child Support Account. Your reasons for deviating might, at first, appear unusual to the court, as most judges in the country will not have encountered parents who wish to use a Child Support

Account. Normally, the judge only hears excuses and pleas from parents wanting the court to deviate upwards or downwards from Guidelines, depending on whether they are paying or receiving. The sample language stresses that you and the other parent are a United Front! You might wish to add some icing to the cake by stating that, if you are permitted to use the Child Support Account, your children will actually receive more support from both of you, because of the additional bonus–that your children will not experience the parental bickering that more typically goes on regarding child support.

Do not allow the court to tell you that a deviation is never permitted. The U.S. Department of Child Support Enforcement, while not enthusiastic about deviations from the state Guidelines, does instruct state courts to consider deviations "…in unusual circumstances." Here is what the Federal Office of Child Support Enforcement advises in its publication (reproduced at their website), titled *"Essentials for Attorneys in Child Support Enforcement,"* when seeking deviations from the Guidelines:

> **"Deviations from Support Guidelines.** The issue of when deviation from Guidelines is appropriate poses a challenge for States. Too many bases for deviation undermine the effectiveness of standard calculations; yet, some flexibility is necessary to prevent inappropriate orders where unusual circumstances exist. While the standard guideline calculation addresses the basic needs of a child, deviation criteria tailor the order to meet the needs of a specific child or children. When a deviation is made, Federal law requires that the decision-maker must make findings on the record that '…state the amount of support that would have been required under the Guidelines and include a justification of why the order varies from the Guidelines.' The standard is the best interest (sic) of the child. Some States, such as Delaware, provide little guidance to the decision-maker by way of deviation criteria. Others, such as Florida, provide detailed and specific Guidelines on what constitutes the basis for deviation." [27]

Obviously, there is no mention of the Child Support Account as a reason to deviate, so you may need to be persistent and firm, when submitting your documents. However, the regulations cited above clearly indicate that the standard to be applied in considering whether the court will allow a deviation is "the best interests of the child." When two parents are standing in court telling a judge they wish to use the Child Support Account and have included all the detail that is set forth in the recommended language, it is usually difficult for a judge to find that such cooperation is not in the best interests of a child. In our experience, since 1983, in mediating the Child Support Account, we have encountered less than a handful of judges or child support magistrates who have denied clients' use of the Account. If you find that your assigned judge is unwilling to grant a deviation, you can respectfully remind the judge that federal law permits deviations from the Guidelines, so long as the reasons for deviating are stated and the deviation provides for the child's best interests *(Please see Chapter 7 for more detailed advice, if your particular court resists granting a deviation for you to use the Child Support Account).*

STEP FOUR: INCLUDE THE BUDGET (TABLE 5-1) THAT THE TWO OF YOU HAVE JOINTLY CREATED

Include a complete budget of shared children's expenses and display it in the section that comes after the section on "Incomes." In many ways, the budget is the central part of the Child Support Account. It is the engine that propels you into the future. All amounts listed are your best estimate of what it will cost the two of you to pay for your children's expenses each month. Take time with the other parent to discuss each line-item. You cannot be exact, and sometimes, unexpected events will impact the budget and require change, going forward. Your child might come to need special tutoring in the future, but at the time of creating the budget, you do not know exactly what that will cost. In such cases, you can simply put in the shared column "50% / 50%", or 60% / 40%, or whatever represents your proportional contributions for those costs.

One parent may have been the bill-payor during the marital relationship and have more knowledge about what has been spent in the past and what will likely be needed in the future. Your goal is to establish agreement, as best as you can, about what it will likely cost in the future to give your children what they need. The task of staying on track does require some regular communication, but you can decide jointly how often you will talk with each other. Surprisingly, there appears to be little risk that the interaction between parents regarding the budget will sour to the point of constant nitpicking and conflict. Rather, just the opposite seems to occur, and more cooperation seems to be generated between parents.

The reason that most parents can successfully cooperate when using the Child Support Account has to do with the shared responsibility that is created. The joint, cooperative discussions of parents begin to revolve around budget choices that they regularly have faced. This is a seismic shift from the current child support system, which places all responsibility on the shoulders of just one parent to try to make the support dollars stretch far enough, never knowing whether it will be enough to cover their children's actual expenses each month. And, when using the Guidelines approach, parental interactions often include accusations, such as: "Why can't you make the court-ordered amount work?! That is what the court ordered me to pay you, and you still ask me for more!" In contrast, when using the Child Support Account, the discussions sound more like this: "We need to revisit the budget, because I have just learned that our oldest has been asked to move up to the travelling basketball team, and it will cost us an additional $850 for registration, travel and other costs."

It is best to include the entire budget in the body of the document that you will be submitting to the court, rather than attaching it at the end, as an exhibit. This is the same budget to which you were introduced in Chapter Three. It follows the same parents and their situation, in which Dad earns $65,000 and Mom earns $39,000. The Minnesota Child Support Guidelines calculator computed the amount of child support that Dad would send to Mom as $144 per month, based upon having two minor children, and following equal timesharing. This is the budget they created in mediation. And, in reaching the $144 child support figure, the only fact of significance within the Guidelines is that Dad was having the children's health insurance coverage deducted from his salary, at the rate of $234 per month.

The following budget, using this format, would be inserted into the actual court documents, and it would be placed right after the draft language on Pg. 55.

Table 5-1. Children's Monthly Expenses

Expense Item	Paid Separately by Dad	Shared	Paid Separately by Mom
Food and groceries	250		250
Eating out	150		150
Lunches at School		85	
Clothing		110	
Cell Phones		60	
Medical Insurance for the two children [If deducted from a paycheck, show who pays]	Deducted from Dad's paycheck	234	
Uncovered medical		34	
Uncovered dental		5	
Uncovered medication prescriptions		20	
Orthodontia		0	
Eyeglasses/Contact Lenses		35	
Car Insurance - daughter		110	
Dance (Costumes/Competition Costs)		250	
School Supplies & Backpacks		20	
Tutoring		127	
Sports (Soccer equipment, fees, and camp)		69	
Haircuts/ Hair Care		40	
Personal care items (cosmetics/other drugstore items)		45	
Gifts for friends' birthday parties		12	
TOTAL Expenses Anticipated to be Paid Separately by Each Parent: [Items with a zero are also considered to be shared if and when they are incurred]	400		400
TOTAL Shared Expenses for their children: [Items with a zero are also considered to be shared if and when they are incurred]		1,256	
Shared Costs Paid by Each [63%-37%]: [For example, if Dad earns $65k annual income and Mom earns $39k annual income, Dad's 63% of $1,256 is $791, and Mom's 37% of $1,256 is $465]	791		465
Credit for Medical Insurance Paid Directly by Dad:	-234		
Monthly Amount Deposited into Account by Each:	557		465

The final sentence that we suggest you place at the end of the budget re-states the obvious, but it always seems appropriate to close the budgets section with a summary about the purpose of the "paid separately columns" and the "shared" columns.

> Each parent shall pay separately for food, recreation, entertainment and travel expenses, which will not be shared as a part of the joint account arrangement.

STEP FIVE: EXPLAIN HOW YOU WILL IMPLEMENT CHANGES

Describe how and when you will change your contributions to the Account and how you will change expense amounts or add categories of new expenses of the children:

> From time to time, and at least once every 12 months, the parents will meet and review the budgeted expenses for their children. At such review, they may add new categories of expenses and may revise current expenditure levels. Upon a substantial change in either of their incomes, they shall also adjust their pro-rata contributions to the Account. In February of each year, they will exchange W-2 income verification or tax returns, in order to adjust their pro-rata contribution towards their children's joint account. Should there be any dispute about the amounts of their respective current gross incomes, they will submit the dispute to a mutually agreed upon C.P.A. or professional family mediator.

This is a very important paragraph. *Not only does it reflect the reality that children's expenses will change over time*. It also shows that you have given some thought to appointing a neutral, expert professional to help you if you are self-employed parents who have a dispute about incomes, or, if one has a salary and benefits that include perks, bonuses, commissions, royalties, dividends, and other types of unusual income. Essentially, you are telling the court that you expect to revisit both the budget and your incomes, because very few people these days have incomes that never change.

STEP SIX: PROMISE TO KEEP YOUR SPENDING WITHIN THE BUDGET PROJECTIONS

> Mom and Dad agree that neither will spend from the joint account for items other than the above authorized categories. Should there be extraordinary and unusual expenses for their children that have not been anticipated and not part of their projected expenses, they agree first to meet and discuss whether or not to incur the expense, and, if they agree, the item will be paid from the joint account.

The above language is really straightforward and common sense. The whole concept of the Child Support Account fails if you go out and purchase an expensive 12-speed racing bike and claim it was part of the $40 per month enrichment budget line item. Those types of bikes can cost thousands of dollars and usually enrichment relates to lower-cost expenses, like piano lessons, books, and perhaps an optional field trip through a club at school. Common sense must prevail, and when common sense is not used, the person not in violation will usually ask for a termination of the use of the Account.

STEP SEVEN: INDICATE THAT THE COURT WILL *NOT* SERVE AS THE MANAGER OF THE ACCOUNT, AND THE *ONLY* ROLE OF THE COURT IS TO REINSTITUTE THE GUIDELINES CHILD SUPPORT IF EITHER OF YOU CHOOSES TO TERMINATE USE OF THE ACCOUNT, FOR ANY REASON

Finally, the language calls for closing with a promise that you will not call upon the court to step in and supervise your use of the Child Support Account. You agree that either parent may choose to terminate the Child Support Account at any time and for any reason, if ever the Child Support Account is no longer working for you. You will then be required to follow your state Guidelines (Use of the Account is *entirely voluntary*).

> In the event that either parent determines that the joint account becomes impractical, or is working unsatisfactorily, either may declare that this arrangement is terminated. They shall then first return to mediation, or, in the event mediation does not result in agreement, to court, to establish a different child support arrangement.

This final paragraph relieves the court of concerns about having to spend countless hours of its resources in hearings to determine if one of you violated the terms of the Child Support Account. This is *really important,* as courts do not want to get into the business of managing numerous child support accounts. The reason that courts rely upon the Guidelines formulas is that these set-formulas reduce child support to something very simple and easy to rule upon. However, the reality is that child support is quite complex, given the need to balance resources and decide what their children need and do not need, across 15 to 20 categories of expenses, and still be able to keep the entire restructured family functioning between two separate homes.

Please see the last section of this book for a complete compilation of all sample language combined in the order that you would submit to court.

Chapter Six:
Variations of the Child Support Account

A very small number of parents who really like the detailed nature of the Child Support Account, may not wish to have a joint account with the other parent. This is understandable, particularly if the parents have had problems in the past with managing joint accounts, with bankruptcies and overdrafts, or, if they simply do not want to have their name associated with the other parent on any joint bank account. Sometimes, either or both parents may not be able to qualify for a bank account, due to low or no income, or because of past credit difficulties. In some cases, they have been living apart for some time before formally filing for divorce, and they do not wish to be constrained by the Guidelines formulas. They might have fallen into a pattern whereby one has been paying for the car insurance and health insurance, and the other has been purchasing clothing and paying for music lessons. Perhaps one parent is with the children less often and is informally sending $400 per month to the other parent, to balance the costs for extra meals and the extra driving that the more-time parent incurs. A variation of the Child Support Account can usually be created and explained in the child support section of the agreements, to convince the court to allow them to continue handling child support by using their own standard of fairness. However, it is important that, initially, care is taken to state what the Guidelines would have required, had the parents wished to follow them.

For the rare cases in which parents choose to customize the standard approach of the Child Support Account, **there are three variations:**

1) Each parent pays directly to the vendors for all purchased items in the budget table, and no money is exchanged between the parents. (Sometimes called "Direct Payments of Children's Expenses") (See Table 6-1);

2) Some payment of child support is transferred from one parent to the other, but the payment is more, or is less, than what the Guidelines would require, and one or both parents also are making other direct payments as outlined in the budget (See Table 6-2);

3) Full payment of Guidelines child support is made, but the budget explains how the child support is to be used . We designate this as "Basic Child Support Under the Guidelines," with an explanation of its intended use (See Table 6-3).

The tables included with each variation are set forth as *examples only,* with details regarding the responsibilities of each parent. All tables track the same set of parents, using the same budgets. They have two children and, as you will recall from the earlier discussion, Father earns more than Mother. Father pays for the children's health insurance from his payroll deductions, and, except for Variation #3, the parents are following an equal time-sharing arrangement.

Please note that the data in Variation #3 (Table 6-3) assume that the children are with Mother 80% of the time [292 days] throughout the year. This example shows how the Account might work with a pattern of unequal parenting time, resulting in Mother receiving $974 of Guidelines child support when the facts of our case used throughout this book were calculated using Minnesota Child Support Guidelines. Were they to have equal time-sharing, *Mother would receive only $144 dollars of child support.* This is an example of how the Guidelines generate unnecessary custody battles, since under the Minnesota Child Support Calculator, in contrast, Mother would receive almost a thousand dollars per month in child support. Nevertheless, for parents who choose to, or are ordered to follow the Guidelines, it is still wise to identify for what the $974 monthly child support is to be used.

These variations always include the budget expense grids, which explain what expenses the basic child support covers and which items need further discussion. Whether the child support amount is more, or less, or equal to the Guidelines, we still suggest that parents include a budget grid with language that says: "Generally, the parent who receives monthly child support payments shall use the amount for the following categories of expenses of their children, in the approximate monthly amounts as set forth in the table below" (Table 6-3).

VARIATION #1: NO CHILD SUPPORT IS EXCHANGED – CHILDREN'S EXPENSES ARE PAID DIRECTLY TO VENDORS BY EITHER PARENT

This method has no monthly child support paid by one parent to the other, but instead each parent pays separately and directly for specific, itemized expenses of their children. Table 6-1 shows who will pay for what. There is no direct exchange of money passing between the parents, but they have an agreement about what each is responsible for paying, even when their children may not be with them (e.g. health insurance can be paid by either parent at any time). While this arrangement can work with any set of parents, it can also work well when parents live in different states, and their children spend summers with one parent, and school years with the other parent.

Table 6-1: Each parent pays designated expenses of their children directly, as set forth in their respective columns. They promise each other that they will each pay for items at the approximate amount as set forth in the table. Notice that there is nothing placed in the shared column. Each set of parents will have a different history as to what has worked for them in the past, and often this purchasing pattern of who pays for what will continue after the separation or divorce.

Table 6-1: No exchange of child support dollars between parents.
(Direct Payment to Vendors of Children's Expenses)

Table 6-1. Children's Monthly Expenses

Expense Item	Paid Separately by Dad	Shared	Paid Separately by Mom
Food and groceries	On own		On own
Eating out	On own		On own
Lunches at School			85
Clothing			110
Cell Phones	60		
Medical Insurance for the two children [Deducted from Dad's paycheck]	234		
Uncovered medical	34		
Uncovered dental	5		
Uncovered medication prescriptions	20		
Orthodontia	Zero Now		
Eyeglasses/Contact Lenses	35		
Car Insurance - daughter	110		
Dance (Costumes/Competition Costs)			250
School Supplies & Backpacks			20
Tutoring for 13-year-old	127		
Sports (Soccer equipment, fees, and camp)	69		
Haircuts/ Hair Care	40		
Personal care items (cosmetics/other drugstore items)	45		
Gifts for friends' birthday parties	12		
TOTAL Expenses Anticipated to be Paid Separately by Each Parent: [Paid from their own separate funds]	791		465

Many parents have said, "Can't we each just pay for what the kids need when they are with us?" For those parents who are engaging in equal time-sharing of their children and have equivalent incomes, the Guidelines in most states call for no, or little, exchange of child support, provided they are equally sharing the medical and day care costs. However, many parents with equal incomes and equal time with their children may still want to use a budget, as set forth above, to make sure they are sharing their children's expenses equivalently or proportionally, and that there is agreement about what expenses each is assuming. Many couples will agree that, in the event that uncovered medical costs become catastrophic, they will start sharing the costs above some agreed-upon level because, technically, the above budget has Father paying 100% of all uncovered medical, with no upper limit, before Mother would have to share the costs. In the above case, they might agree that Dad will pay the first $1,000 of uncovered medical, dental, and other medically related expenses incurred each year that are not covered by insurance. Thereafter, all uncovered medical costs would be shared proportionally.

VARIATION #2: SOME PAYMENT OF CHILD SUPPORT IS MADE – WITH EACH PARENT PAYING CERTAIN ITEMIZED EXPENSES DIRECTLY TO THE VENDORS

In Budget Table 6-2, some amount of child support is paid (often a downward deviation amount), and additional support is provided in the form of payments directly to vendors, and/or additional payments sent to the recipient of child support, with clarification regarding what that money is to be use for. There may be many reasons why parents agree to this, but it is usually due to the desire of the person paying child support to be able to participate in direct payments, as a part of being a parent, instead of saying to a child, "You must always ask your mom about that; all I do is pay child support."

Table 6-2: A smaller-than-Guidelines-child support payment (This usually is a downward deviation from state Guidelines). In this second example, details show additional payments made by each parent, directly to vendors of child expenses.

Table 6-2. Children's Monthly Expenses

Expense Item	Paid Separately by Dad	Shared	Paid Separately by Mom
Food and groceries	On own		On own
Eating out	On own		On own
Lunches at School			85
Clothing			110
Cell Phones	60		
Medical Insurance for the two children [Deducted from Dad's paycheck]	234		
Uncovered medical	34	34	
Uncovered dental	5	5	
Uncovered medication prescriptions	20		
Orthodontia	Proportional		
Eyeglasses/Contact Lenses		35	
Car Insurance - daughter	110		
Dance (Costumes/Competition Costs)			250
School Supplies & Backpacks			20
Tutoring for 13-year-old	127		
Sports (Soccer equipment, fees, and camp)	69		
Haircuts/ Hair Care			40
Personal care items (cosmetics/other drugstore items)			45
Gifts for friends' birthday parties			12
TOTAL Expenses Anticipated to be Paid Separately by Each Parent: [Paid from their own separate funds]	**659**		**562**

The Father, in this example, would pay the Mother $400 per month as child support, which is less than the $974 per month calculated by the Minnesota Guidelines when unequal time sharing occurs. However, he also would pay, separately and directly to vendors, for other specific expenses of their children, such as their child's car insurance and other items in his column, for a total of

$659. This would result in the father providing more in total support dollars than would be required by the Guidelines. Parents may have their own reasons for wanting a parent to pay some expenses directly, instead of sending the child support for the other parent to make the payment or instead of running the funds through the Child Support Account. In the example in Table 6-2, the parents decided that they wanted to use the Child Support Account for shared medical expenses which can be paid by either, resulting in a record being kept through the Child Support Account statements. Mother then will be responsible for the expenses of dance and other items in her column, and Father will then be responsible for the auto insurance expenses of the child and other items in his column.

These types of situations, which combine direct payment, sharing of uncovered medical expenses, and smaller than Guidelines payments, usually are utilized by parents who have been separated for some time and have found that informally they have been handling the children's expenses in the above manner and wish to continue doing it the same way that has worked for them in the past.

VARIATION #3: FULL GUIDELINES CHILD SUPPORT IS PAID, BUT WITH ADDITIONAL LANGUAGE DETAILING THE SPECIFIC ITEMS FOR WHICH THE CHILD SUPPORT WILL GENERALLY BE USED.

Table 6-3 shows parental agreement that the required amount of Guidelines child support will be paid each month. More importantly, the agreement is about what the support is to be used for. This helps both the payor and the recipient of support, because it shows exactly which expenses of the children are being funded by the "basic" support payment. Parents can also use the grid to demonstrate agreement about future expected expenses, such as orthodontia or an agreed-upon cell phone cost, as a child reaches a certain age. At future reviews, other line items might be added, such as agreements about how they will share the costs of car insurance for a teen or how they will share the educational/college costs of a 19-year-old. This is important because few State Child Support Guidelines address future changes, nor do they reach anywhere near the level of detail as presented in these tables.

Of course, it is not possible to foresee all future one-time expenses, such as a summer sport camp, a need for tutoring, or other unexpected expenses. Yet, when parents rely on the budget of expenses as a tool for their discussions about their children, they become clear about child support, which also helps to keep the children out of the middle of such discussions and keeps the parents out of court.

Table 6-3: Guidelines child support amount of $974 per month is paid, showing how it is intended to be used.

Table 6-3. Children's Monthly Expenses			Paid Separately by Mom from Child Support of $974 per month
Expense Item	**Paid Separately by Dad**	**Shared**	
Food and groceries	90		360
Eating out	200		100
Lunches at School			85
Clothing			110
Cell Phones			60
Medical Insurance for the two children [Deducted from Dad's paycheck]	234		
Uncovered medical		34	
Uncovered dental		5	
Uncovered medication prescriptions		20	
Orthodontia		0	
Eyeglasses/Contact Lenses		35	
Car Insurance - daughter	110		
Dance (Costumes/Competition Costs)			250
School Supplies & Backpacks			20
Tutoring for 13-year-old	127		
Sports (Soccer equipment, fees, and camp)			69
Haircuts/ Hair Care			40
Personal care items (cosmetics/other drugstore items)			45
Gifts for friends' birthday parties			12
TOTAL Expenses Anticipated to be Paid Separately by Each Parent: [Paid from their own separate funds]	**761**		**1,151**

In the above example in Table 6-3, the Minnesota Guidelines amount of child support calls for $974 per month if Mom has approximately 80% of the overnights. They agree that Father's $974 payment as child support each month to Mother shall, as a general rule, be used to pay for items in Mother's column of expenses, and, in addition, they will share proportionally all uncovered medical costs. This detailed approach can be helpful, because it allows for both parents to understand how the child support sent by Father to Mother is being used. If a new expense of a child is incurred, the parents can address that new expense in light of what each is responsible for paying at the time the new child expense arises. We have found that the parent expected to pay child support loves this concept, since that parent now understands what the child support will be for, and it will not directly benefit the other parent–only the children.

Some parents have started out using the Child Support Account and find that, after some passage of time, they each fall into patterns of being responsible for certain recurring categories. Do not hesitate to meet with the other parent and make whatever adjustments you need. Indeed, one of the most useful aspects of the Child Support Account is what we call its self-modification principle. Existing Guidelines require parents to regularly spend money to go back to court to modify support each time there is a substantial change in incomes or in parenting time. This return to court is required because the Support and Collections agencies will not accept a voluntary change in child support, even if both parents agree, unless it is also accompanied by a new Court Order approving the change. When using the Child Support Account, parents will meet at least once a year to review, update, and to change the budget and their respective monthly contributions, if their incomes have changed.

When using the Child Support Account after being granted a deviation from the Guidelines, you do not need to obtain any kind of court permission to make voluntary changes in the direct payments. In fact, it is expected that, on your own, you periodically will make changes when your children's expenses and needs change or when your own incomes change. It is important for parents to record, sign, and date all agreed-upon changes that they make in the budget and in their monthly contributions to the Account. We suggest that parents always record these changes when they occur and each keep copies, because there may be a time in the future when, for example, the changes are not remembered or when there is a remarriage, and the new spouse questions why the amount is so different from the original agreement.

In addition, to be on the safe side, both of you should return to court if you both decide to reduce or eliminate the child support transfer under one of these three variations, because if the receiver of child support has a change of heart and decides it was wrong to reduce or eliminate the court-ordered transfer payment of child support, you could find yourself on the hook for child support arrears that were informally forgiven without modifying the original child support court order. The safest rule to follow is that, if you decide to use one of these hybrid variations described in this chapter, you are still technically under the jurisdiction of the court regarding the child support transfer payment, and you should take time to modify the court order if you informally change the amount transferred between the two of you.

When you have obtained permission to use the Child Support Account and no actual child support dollars are being exchanged, you do not have to get approval from the court, since you are essentially on your own. Either the account will work well, or you can decide to end it.

A number of years ago, we received a call from a mom who indicated that we had mediated their divorce settlement five years earlier. She worried that she and the father would be guilty of contempt of court if they stopped following the order requiring use of the Account. Her first question was, "Do we have to go to court if we decide we do not wish to continue using the Account?" Our first thought was she might be experiencing difficulties and wanted to institute the Guidelines. As our conversation continued, it turned out that, contrary to the arrangement described in the original court order of their divorce settlement, she had begun to assume responsibility for purchasing the children's clothing and paying for lunch tickets and extracurricular activities, including dance lessons for the girls. She said that Dad began paying for the medical insurance and all uncovered medical and dental costs, as well as the insurance, maintenance, and gas for the car that is used by their 17-year-old. She continued by saying that using the Account seemed to be working well, and it was balanced, considering both of their incomes. We responded by pointing out that since there was no payment of child support in their decree of dissolution, there could be no possibility of any arrears occurring. They had the language for reservation of child support in their original agreement and also in their divorce decree, developed six years earlier. We assured her that the detailed language about using the Account is there as a guide, and if they choose to deviate, they can do so on their own. We also encouraged her to record the changes and for each to sign and date the record in the event that their memories were not as reliable in the future.

Her phone call was a reminder that, because the use of the Account is an entirely voluntary, self-regulated replacement for the existing state Guidelines support, a parent would not seek to hold the other parent in contempt for violating a part of the agreement. A dad would not file a motion in Court demanding that Mom be held in contempt of court for failing to pay for the dance and piano lessons, as agreed to in their Child Support Account. If a problem were to arise, the remedy is first to confer with each other and try to reach new agreements on their own, or if needed, to return to mediation. If that is unsuccessful, then simply terminate the use of the Account and obtain a court order establishing the Guidelines and mandatory wage withholding. One reason that you probably cannot rely on the courts to enforce the details of the Child Support Account is the court's inability to wade into the minefield of overseeing thousands of bank accounts, which would require adding hundreds of new staff. Think of the Child Support Account as your informal tool that works better than the Guidelines. If you and your co-parent cannot make it work, you two are probably not candidates to continue using it since no judge will be able to magically coerce the other parent to stop misusing the Account.

While using the Child Support Account, parents can modify their arrangements at any time, provided they both agree. Unlike the Child Support and Collections System, they will not be building up any arrears unless they both agree that one of them has fallen behind in their contributions. Only if the Account is no longer working, according to their particular definition of that, will a return to court possibly be needed. That return would then require a request to the court for a termination of the Child Support Account and commencement of the Guidelines formula, with court-ordered wage-withholding and all the sanctions that apply for non-payment. When a mom once asked, in a mediation session, "What would happen if he stopped putting his check into the Account?" Before answering, Dad responded, "I would be a fool to do that and risk having my employer complain to me about needing to start wage-withholding on my paycheck in order to send the money to support and collections, and that's not even counting the cost of returning to court to establish the proper Guidelines support amount!"

The best rule is that, if you find that the Child Support Account or any of the three variations discussed above is no longer working for you, take some immediate action, either by requesting an immediate return to mediation to fix the problem jointly, or a return to Court if you find no cooperation from the other parent. This suggestion is consistent with the understanding that the use of the Child Support Account is entirely voluntary. It is understandable that if courts are hesitant to approve deviations from Guidelines, do not expect them to untangle things if use of the Account proves unsatisfactory for you. You should not let the problems continue and then expect some court to fix it, because remember your promise to the court was to abandon the use of the Account and revert to the Guidelines. Perhaps, someday in the future, other states may adopt a form of the Minnesota Statute,[28] that permits parents who have adopted a parenting plan "to allocate expenses between them," and have the court treat the allocation as an enforceable contract between them.

Chapter Seven:

Getting Court Approval for a Deviation from Guidelines

Some of what follows in this chapter has been presented earlier, in Chapter Three, but the information is so important that it will be helpful to review it again. In addition, this chapter provides some background information about the source of the resistance, as well as guidance on how to obtain a deviation from the child support Guidelines.

In the documents that you submit to the court, you will ask the court to approve a "deviation" from the Guidelines, and you will be assuring the judge that, if your Child Support Account does not work, you will then accept a new court order that requires both of you to follow your state's Child Support Guidelines.

If you encounter strong resistance from the court, remind the Judge that the federal Family Support Act of 1988 does allow all states' courts to deviate from the Guidelines. There are basically two reasons why the court makes it difficult for you to deviate from the Guidelines and replace the Guidelines formula with the Child Support Account:

1. Courts anticipate (incorrectly) that the Child Support Account is a risky idea that is likely to land you back in court, once you fail; and,

2. Each state's court system and affiliated child support collection agencies receives a good deal of money from the federal government as reimbursement funds to run the courts. When Guidelines child support is ordered to be paid through wage-withholding that is managed by departments of support and collections, the amount of federal reimbursement dollars they receive is tied to their collection rate, as well as to the number of people who use support and collections.

Most people are not aware of the fact that for each dollar collected through the various state support and collections agencies, significant funds are reimbursed to each state to help them run their court system. The Family Support Act of 1988 was originally designed as a way to collect money from an absent parent who fails to support a child, which results in the taxpayer having to foot the bill. Generally referred to as Title IV-D of the Social Security Act, this law was expanded to serve all parents with a child support order, not just those receiving welfare assistance. The federal government reimburses the states 67% (two dollars for every three dollars spent) for the cost of providing these support collection services.[29]

But, there is even more good news for the guardians of the state treasuries. Based upon a state's child support collection success rate, they are given added incentive bonuses above the 67% rate.[30] Thus, if courts were to allow too many people to start using the Child Support Account and opt out of having their child support collected through support and collections agencies, the federal reimbursement to each state would diminish dramatically. It can be said that you help fund the courts every time you pay your child support through support and collections.

The judge also worries that you are doing the wrong thing by embracing such a non-traditional idea as a joint Child Support Account. Judges often view most parents as incapable of cooperating with each other after a divorce or a separation. Remember, the court has established a contest (adversarial) system for you because of the mistaken belief that, if you cannot raise your children together in the same home, you cannot possibly raise your children in separate homes. Therefore, it is necessary to put one of you in charge (custody) and require wage-withholding from the less-worthy, visiting parent, and that he (or, sometimes she) send it to the more worthy (custodial) parent. On the other hand, the Child Support Account assumes a modest measure of cooperation and sharing–something that most separated parents desire. To suddenly see parents standing in court telling the judge that they wish to share the costs of their children, using a joint account, creates deep concern on the part of many judges and hearing officers.

To increase your chances of obtaining permission for a deviation, you will need to explain in your paperwork to the court that your request to deviate from the Guidelines need not be permanent. In the event that you find the Child Support Account does not work satisfactorily for either parent, you promise to revert back to the Guidelines at that time. Tell the court you will always jointly support your children, but you just want an opportunity to use the Child Support Account, because it is in the best interests of your children, and it is seen as fairer by both of you.

Keep in mind that any resistance by the court that you encounter has nothing to do with you. It is all about satisfying the court's need to comply with the Federal Government's efforts to collect money from an absent parent who is not supporting their children and to raise money to pay for its child support enforcement and collection efforts. The government policy makers believe that deadbeat parents cost taxpayers a great deal of money when government has to give welfare dollars to the other needy parent who, presumably, is raising their children "alone."

For Never-Married Parents Who Are Not in Conflict, But Living Apart, You May Use the Child Support Account Without Asking for Court Permission, Because You Are Not Subject to the Court

There is a growing number of never-married parents who decide to separate and request assistance in mediating a parenting plan and child support. These parents are not subject to the Court's jurisdiction (power). Many of these parents successfully use the Child Support Account, and at the conclusion of mediation, they decide there is no reason to go to court just to get the support and collections agencies involved in their lives. More importantly, there is no reason to ask the court to approve what they already know works for them. They are not expecting to be receiving welfare in the future, they have not married, so they do not need to obtain a divorce decree, and they decide to successfully conclude mediation, with copies of their parenting plan and Child Support Account agreements and without ever appearing in court. Most people would like to avoid court whenever possible. And, there are increasing numbers of never-married parents living separately who work out parenting plans and share support of their children without ever setting foot in a courthouse.

Be Detailed About Your Reasons for Deviating

After you set forth what your state Guidelines would require, the next step is to be very detailed about why you are deviating from the Guidelines. Here you don't say that you will not send child support, but you do say that *you both are choosing to support your children in a different manner.* Basically, you are saying that you do not wish to have one of you send child support money to the other but that you *both* will support your children by sending support money directly to the Child Support Account, which, in turn, is used to support your children.

You may use the sample language we have provided in Chapter 5 that shows your reasons for deviating. These reasons have successfully been accepted by the courts in several states. The reasons for deviating include the fact that by using the Child Support Account, children are kept out of the middle of parental conflicts, and that using the Child Support Account is in the children's best interests. Keep in mind that your reason for deviating might at first appear unusual to the court, as most judges in the country will not have encountered parents who wish to use the Child Support Account. Normally, the judge only hears excuses and pleas from parents wanting the court to deviate upwards or downwards from the Guidelines, depending on whether they are paying or receiving. The sample language stresses that you and the other parent are a United Front in gaining an amicable parting!

Do not allow the court to tell you that a deviation is never permitted. The U.S. Department of Child Support Enforcement, while not enthusiastic about deviations from the state Guidelines, does instruct state courts to consider deviations "…in unusual circumstances." The Federal Office of Child Support Enforcement, in its publication, *"Essentials for Attorneys in Child Support Enforcement,"* advises the following for those seeking deviation from the Guidelines:

> **Deviations from Support Guidelines.** The issue of when deviation from Guidelines is appropriate poses a challenge for States. Too many bases for deviation undermine the effectiveness of standard calculations; yet, some flexibility is necessary to prevent inappropriate orders where unusual circumstances exist. While the standard guideline calculation addresses the basic needs of a child, deviation criteria tailor the order to meet the needs of a specific child or children. When a deviation is made, Federal law requires that the decision-maker must make findings on the record that "state the amount of support that would have been required under the Guidelines and include a justification of why the order varies from the Guidelines." The standard is the best interest (sic) of the child. Some States, such

as Delaware, provide little guidance to the decision-maker by way of deviation criteria. Others, such as Florida, provide detailed and specific Guidelines on what constitutes the basis for deviation. [31]

Obviously, there is no mention of the Child Support Account as a reason to deviate, so you may need to be persistent and firm when submitting your documents. However, the regulations cited above clearly indicate that the standard to be applied in considering whether the court will allow a deviation is "the best interests of the child." In our experience, when two parents are standing in court telling a judge that they wish to use the Child Support Account and have included all the detail that is set forth in the recommended language herein, it is usually difficult for a judge to find that such cooperation is not in the best interests of a child. In our experience mediating the Child Support Account since 1983, we have encountered less than a handful of judges or child support officials who question the use of the Account. In those cases, you can respectfully disagree and remind the judge that federal law permits deviations from the Guidelines, so long as the reasons for deviating are stated and the deviation provides for the child's best interests.

Some states provide detailed guidance on this; other states provide very little in the way of explaining exceptions.

In our experience, you have the best chance of convincing your judge or child support official to allow deviation from state Guidelines if you include the following "reasons for deviating" in your settlement documents:

> The parents prefer to use this method of sharing the costs of raising their children, rather than one parent sending a sum of money to the other, because this direct payment of children's expenses from a joint account accomplishes the following:
>
> (a) Permits both parents to pay for items that their children need when their children are with that parent, instead of telling their children they must ask the recipient of child support to be the one to always purchase necessary items for them;

(b) Provides for the parents to keep a record of expenses incurred by their children, or on their behalf, thereby allowing the parents to more easily make future modifications of the Child Support Account, as children's expenses change in the future;

(c) Unlinks child support from time with the children, thereby separating the discussions of parenting time-sharing from discussions of the child support amounts, and the confounding effects on the resolutions of both issues;

(d) Allows for periodic adjustments to child support by modifying the amount that each parent regularly deposits into the Account, upon their review of changes in each parent's income;

(e) Is a continuation of the ordinary and familiar joint consultation and decision-making that naturally takes place between the parents during their marriage (and/or during their separation);

(f) Is consistent with the parents' choice to mediate their divorce, which is evidenced by their shared parenting plan, that requires them to share (proportionally or equally) in the costs of raising their children.

The parents believe that it is in their children's best interests to reserve the issue of child support and permit the sharing of expenses as provided above.

The above-suggested language has worked well in Minnesota courts. A careful reading of the variations rules of all 50 states will show that the one principle they have in common is that the deviation from Guidelines is for "best interests of the children." You may find yourself standing in court telling a judge that allowing both of you to try the Child Support Account will more likely produce or improve parental cooperation. You will also promise that if the Child Support Account does not work for the two of you, you agree to revert to the state Guidelines.

Nevertheless, your best response to the court is that the Child Support Account is in your children's best interests because the detailed nature of it shows that the parents have given considerable thought and energy to creating its terms. It would be unlikely that after all the work of creating the budgets and agreeing to deviate from the Guidelines, one of the parents would just walk away from it.

One of the peculiar aspects of divorce is that your Marital Termination Agreement is the only contract you will ever sign that must first be pre-approved by a judge. All other contracts end up before a judge only if there is some dispute about its interpretation or if there is a claim that one of the parties has not adhered to the conditions of the contract.

BE CLEAR THAT YOU ARE GIVING YOURSELF AND THE OTHER PARENT A BAILOUT IF THE ARRANGEMENT DOES NOT WORK AT SOME POINT IN THE FUTURE

Your request to deviate from the Guidelines will have a greater chance of approval if you include what we call a "bailout provision." This allows the judge to conclude that you are not permanently rejecting the Guidelines, but just that you are putting the Guidelines on the shelf while using the Child Support Account. In most states, you do this by "reserving" the Guidelines method of child support.

In the final analysis, you will be showing the court that you have provided for the care and support of your children, but you are just doing it differently from the Guidelines formula followed in each state.

EXPANDED LANGUAGE CONCERNING TERMINATION OF THE CHILD SUPPORT ACCOUNT

The following is expanded sample language stating you will not return to court to request help with making the Child Support Account work. You promise to seamlessly transition to use the Guidelines and the support and collections apparatus if you find that continued use of the account is not workable or possible.

Sample Language:

> Either parent may, at any time, terminate use of the
> Child Support Account and invoke the automatic
> commencement of the State Child Support Guidelines, by

notifying the other parent in writing, and sending a copy of such letter to the local office of Support and Collections located (Here include address and phone number of your local office). Absent agreement on their own, the parents shall cooperate in returning to professional family mediation, or to their attorneys, or by scheduling an appearance in court before the judge, to establish the amount of child support that shall be collected by support and collections, and paid to the other parent.

Remember, continued use of the Account is voluntary. The court will likely be impressed by your willingness to include a statement regarding termination of its use at any time, if the process is being abused or is simply no longer workable. You need not justify why it did not work for you. Allowing either of you to terminate its use for any reason, and to return to the Guidelines at any time, encourages continued cooperative behavior. Moreover, this removes a possible fear of the judicial officer that he or she might have to figure out a way to enforce the Child Support Account if someone requests the judge to make the other parent adhere to its terms. For example, once a child starts driving and causes the car insurance fees to double, you could not expect to use the court to hold the other parent in contempt of court for failing to agree with you on how much money should be deposited into the Account. If there is any aspect of the Child Support Account that is not working, you must accept the fact that you will revert to using the Guidelines method of child support.

IF THE COURT CONTINUES TO DENY YOUR REQUEST TO DEVIATE FROM GUIDELINES, GET CREATIVE

You could try to get a bill through the legislature permitting voluntary use of the Child Support Account. Below is the statutory reference that we use in the state of Minnesota that provides for allocating children's expenses between the parents. You will not be able to use this in your state, but it is shown here for reference only:

Authority for Deviation: Minnesota State Parenting Plan legislation [518.1705 Subd. 8} states that "(a) parents creating a parenting plan are subject to the

requirements of the child support Guidelines under
Chapter 518A," and that "(b) parents may include in
the parenting plan an allocation of expenses for the
child(ren). The allocation is an enforceable contract
between the parents.

As of this writing, Minnesota is the only state in the country that has this
legislation[32] permitting parents to deviate from Guidelines and create an
enforceable contract between them for allocating funds for their children's
expenses. In 1998, we suggested to Representative Andy Dawkins that we include
the above language for allocating child expenses into the Minnesota Plan Act.
Andy was fully supportive of it. Allowing for direct payments is essentially a
deviation from the Guidelines and consistent with the concept of self-directed
planning. However, in the hearings on the parenting plan legislation, objections
were raised by some committee members that this contract provision would be a
wholesale repeal of the child support Guidelines. To satisfy the objectors and get
the bill out of committee to the floor for a vote, we added section (a), which
assured everyone that, even when parents submitted a parenting plan to the court
in place of designating custody, they still must continue to support their children.

If you reside in a state like Florida, or Texas, or North Dakota, where parents who
wish to use the Child Support Account have found it exceedingly difficult to obtain
approval from the court to follow the Child Support Account in place of the
Guidelines approach, you may wish to include language such as the following,
that directly incorporates concepts from the handbook of the United States Office
of Support and Enforcement, titled *Essentials for Attorneys in Child Support
Enforcement, 3rd Edition*–a manual that instructs attorneys in how to obtain a
deviation from State Guidelines:

Authority for Deviation: The Family Support Act of 1988
allows for deviations to address the special needs of
our children. The budget included herein addresses not
only the basic needs of our child(ren),but is also
specifically tailored to meet the special and
extraordinary needs of our child(ren). The Guidelines
formula that aggregates our child(ren) with every other

child in the state into one formulaic child support result is unlikely to provide fairness to our children or to our family now residing in two separate households. Therefore, we parents, together, respectfully request the court approve our use of the Child Support Account as described more fully herein.

The above sample language takes some of the wording and concepts provided in the previous reference to the "Essentials for Attorneys" handbook from the United States Office of Child Support and Enforcement (footnote 31) and makes it a justifiable request that the parents be allowed to create a Child Support Account mechanism that is special to the needs of only one family.

ADDITIONAL ITEMS TO ADDRESS AND OPTIONALLY INCLUDE IN THE CHILD SUPPORT SECTION, DEPENDING ON YOUR STATE OF RESIDENCE AND ITS LOCAL RULES OF COURTS.

- Tell the judge (or child support official) assigned to your case that you understand what the Guidelines formula amount would be in your own case;

- Tell the court that you intend to deviate from the Guidelines, and that you both will follow the agreements for using the Child Support Account;

- List the reasons as to why you are deviating from the formula and the reasons why such deviation is in the best interests of your children;

- Be complete in reporting the details of the Account, so the Court can see that you have a well-planned budget of children's expenses and that you clearly have put time and thought into the negotiations about child support;

- In addition to the language that creates the Child Support Account and, depending on local legal custom and practice, here is a listing of other typical child support issues that may be needed in your agreements:

  a) In many states, you may need to explicitly state that you will, or will not, include a Cost Of Living Adjustment (COLA) that automatically changes the child support Guidelines when the cost of living statistics (kept by the Bureau of Labor Statistics) are published each year. When using the Child Support Account, you will state that no COLA is needed because under the terms of the Child Support Account, you will be meeting periodically to adjust the budget of your children's expenses, and to change your contributions to the Account, if there are significant changes in either parent's income. Therefore, as parents, you, and not the state, will change your child support arrangements, based upon your actual expenses and incomes, not upon the amount required by the state Guidelines.

b) Some states will want you to indicate explicitly who is responsible for providing the health insurance coverage for your children, if such coverage is available. Even though there is a column in the budget showing which parent is responsible for paying for dependent care coverage, it will be useful to include a paragraph at the end of the Child Support Account that says, "Regardless of which parent provides the health insurance coverage for the minor children, both parents agree that such costs will always be a shared expense."

c) If, during the marriage, life insurance was important to the family and the other parent was a beneficiary, you may choose to use life insurance as a way of replacing lost child support, should one of you die before the child support obligations end. You will need to include a statement of how this will be accomplished. This may be done by designating the surviving parent as the beneficiary of your life insurance, in order to replace the child support amount that you would have paid had you not died, or by creating a trust, to appoint someone to receive your life insurance and then continuing to pay support to the surviving parent.

d) It is also customary to indicate when the child support obligations will end. Check on the local requirements in your state, or in your local jurisdiction, about customary practice. Note that, while not a legal requirement, you may choose to continue child support past a child's 18th birthday or graduation from high school. Many parents continue to use the Child Support Account while their children attend college.

Finally, as has been repeatedly pointed out, make sure you acknowledge that the court has the right to reinstitute the Guidelines if you find that, in the future, the Child Support Account is not working for you and you want the court to order that the Guidelines be implemented in your case.

A NOTE TO USERS OF THIS BOOK:

In this book, we have tried to provide you with the concepts and language of the Child Support Account, so that you may incorporate them into your own divorce document, and begin to experience their benefits. It is up to you to inform yourself about local jurisdictional practices in your own state of residence, regarding different or unexpected requirements or local practices. Nothing of the content in this book is meant to give or provide legal advice. It is offered only as information for you to navigate the child support system on your own terms.

Chapter Eight:
Why The Child Support Account Works So Well

Many who first hear of the Child Support Account wonder whether only cooperative parents will be able to use it. In fact, we have found in our mediation practices that the use of the Account actually *increases* the likelihood of cooperation. This is mainly because it provides an important structure to a commonly unstructured area of contention–dealing with finances during and after a separation or divorce. Cooperative parents, and parents in high conflict, alike, have successfully used the Child Support Account. We believe this is due to the detailed nature of this tool.

Whereas child support Guidelines formulas calculate a fixed amount of money and require the non-custodial parent to pay to the custodial parent, the Child Support Account allows the parents to determine each parent's responsibilities for paying the expenses of their children while keeping a record of those expenses. This eliminates conflict about who is supposed to pay what, and what each dollar will be used for. But, most importantly, the child support amounts are *set by the parents, not by the court.* This creates ownership and acceptance of the plan by both parents and reduces the likelihood of future conflict.

Cooperative behavior is also strengthened when Mom and Dad engage in joint decision-making, as they do when creating the Account. When they discuss and agree upon each particular expense item, they are more likely to arrive at a point where cooperation becomes the norm, and they are more likely to be successful in resolving future cost concerns related to their children. Instead of pitching their case to a judge or to a child support official, parents shift the child support question, from "What are the proper input numbers that they should plug into the court formula?" to a new question. This new question is wholly unrelated to custody, sanctions, and "awards" of child support issued by the court. This shift in focus moves parents from competing to negotiating solutions for their children's needs and expenses. From a common-sense perspective, it is an elegant structural solution to the financial problems associated with raising children in separate residences. Here are the benefits of the Child Support Account:

USING THE ACCOUNT CREATES MUTUALITY AND SHARED RESPONSIBILITY

First, and perhaps most importantly, the Child Support Account puts the burden for making it work squarely on the shoulders of both parents. Use of the Account shifts the focus from asking how much can be obtained from the less-time parent, to jointly planning how both parents' incomes will fund the needs of their children. Both parents are equal negotiators. The task of jointly building a shared budget of children's expenses is entirely different than working with an attorney to try to prove that one parent is entitled to more child support than the other is willing to pay.

SUCCESSFUL USE OF THE ACCOUNT REQUIRES COMMUNICATION BETWEEN THE PARENTS

While challenging, at times, when parents have regular conversations about their children, cooperation becomes the norm. The discussions no longer center on arguing over the amount required by the Guidelines, but rather on the future needs of their children. If there has been extensive past litigation or high conflict, use of the Account may also be a turning point towards re-focusing on their children, rather than focusing all their energy on an adversarial court contest.

THE CHILD SUPPORT ACCOUNT IS PERCEIVED BY BOTH PARENTS AS A FAIRER METHOD THAN USING THE EXISTING CHILD SUPPORT GUIDELINES

Parents who have been the payors of Guidelines child support often make comments such as, "Now I can actually see what my support dollars are being used for." Receivers of child support funds have said, "Now, the other parent will see what it really costs to raise our children." There can be no doubt that a dollar spent from the Account for items in the agreed-upon categories is a dollar that does not end up in being spent on the needs of the other parent. More importantly, there will no longer be the oft-sung refrain: "I wonder what the other parent and his/her "significant other" are doing with all that child support money?"

BOTH PARENTS ARE RECOGNIZED AS SIGNIFICANT PROVIDERS

An important aspect of parenting is in purchasing items for the children. When *both* parents purchase these items, using the Account, children understand that both of their parents are actively involved in making decisions about their needs and helping them get satisfied. For example, important parent-child bonding activities include accompanying the children in buying their shoes and clothes, helping them pick out their first cell phone, and taking them to the barber to have their hair cut. Most parents do not want to limit these bonding experiences to just one parent.

THE ACCOUNT ENCOURAGES PARENTS TO SET ACCEPTABLE LIMITS ON EXPENDITURES FOR THEIR CHILDREN

In accord with the agreements in the Account about spending, when a child asks for a new, costly item, she will be told: "I need to check with your (mom/dad), because your request is not in our budgeted expenses." Or, "Sorry, Kevin, we have already spent our entire budget for this month." As such, both parents now must keep an eye on purchases for their children, because *both* parents (not just the recipient of child support) will take the heat for telling their children, "Unfortunately, we don't have the money for that."

THE ACCOUNT IS SELF-MODIFYING, THEREBY REDUCING COURT VISITS

The Child Support Account eliminates the need to continually return to court to modify child support. Just after the recession of 2009, county courts in Minnesota needed to add numerous part-time child-support magistrates because so many payors of child support hurried to the courthouse seeking a reduction in their support payments due to lost jobs or reductions in income. The cost to the courts of parents returning to court to modify their support obligation each time there is a change in income is significantly reduced when using the Child Support Account. Parents agree, as part of their commitment to use the Account, that they will contribute to it, on a pro-rata basis, according to their incomes (or they will adopt some other fairness principle, based upon their own unique circumstances). Once a year, or in whatever time frame they decide, they exchange income verification and if either or both of their incomes have changed substantially, they will modify their monthly contributions, accordingly.

THE ACCOUNT ELIMINATES COUNTLESS MONTHLY ACCOUNTING ADJUSTMENTS

Child Support Guidelines often require parents to proportionally share the cost of items like daycare or uncovered medical expenses, beyond the amount given for basic support. Parents often struggle with keeping records of who owes what for these items, particularly since one parent may advance the amount and then try to get reimbursement from the other for his or her share. The Child Support Account allows for parents to set aside an agreed-upon amount each month. Then, when it is paid, either by check or with a credit card, there is a record of such payment. More importantly, there is no need to continually make adjustments or reimbursements.

CUSTODY BATTLES ARE AVOIDED

Because the Account unhooks the parenting time factor from the support calculations, there is no need to worry about one more overnight affecting the amount of child support received. Custody is not considered when using the Child Support Account; overnights or days are not obsessively counted, as they are with Child Support Guidelines formulas in use throughout the states.

THE ACCOUNT IS NOT A ONE-SIZE-FITS-ALL APPROACH

Child support Guidelines do not recognize special expenses. Although the statutes behind many state Guidelines allow for upward deviation from the Guidelines, the costs can be substantial for the adversarial contest required to convince a judge to increase child support and make the other parent pay the extra amount. In contrast, the Child Support Account allows a family to plan for unique expenses, such as when a child unexpectedly needs tutoring or has a special musical talent that is costly to support. And, the Account allows for both parents to share these special expenses in whatever proportion they might agree to, or for one parent to pay for them directly.

USING THE ACCOUNT CREATES A GREATER LIKELIHOOD OF MUTUAL COMPLIANCE

Mediators have discovered that people have difficulty violating agreements in which they have participated. There is a world of difference between a judge saying, "I hereby order you to pay $543 per month child support," and two parents saying, "We, together, need to figure out a way to pay for our daughter's orthodontia and our son's counseling."

AND, THERE IS NO RISK!

There is no long-term risk if the Child Support Account does not work for you. If the method fails, parents simply are required to revert back to following the State Guidelines. Should one parent wish to terminate use of the Account, the sample language in Chapter 3 calls for an immediate return to the State Guidelines without having to prove why it didn't work or who caused it to fail. Either parent may request, at any time, *and for any reason,* to end the use of the Account. And, if necessary, they may return to court to determine what the Child Support Guidelines would require and to obtain a court order to that effect. In some courts, if the parents can voluntarily compute and agree upon the Guidelines child support amount, they would be permitted to simply sign and send in a Stipulation for Settlement without a court appearance.

IN SUM, THE CHILD SUPPORT ACCOUNT:

- Unlinks time with the children from child support amounts;
- Creates shared parental responsibility;
- Improves communication between the parents;
- Perceived by parents to be fairer than using the Guidelines;
- Recognizes both parents' financial contributions to their children;
- Provides for more parental control of their children's expenses;
- Can be modified directly by the parents;
- Provides easier accounting of shared contributions;
- Diminishes or eliminates the need for custody contests;
- Is unique to each post-divorce parenting agreement;
- Ensures greater likelihood of compliance with the agreements;
- Carries no risk, if the method fails.

BUT, THE ABSOLUTE BEST PART OF USING THE CHILD SUPPORT ACCOUNT:

You will be better co-parents by presenting a united front to your children when they ask you to buy things for them. Your parenting relationship will be at its best, because you will have preempted conflict over spending money on the needs of your children, and you each will be able to share time with your children without having to worry about its impact on child support!

Chapter Nine:

How the Account Can Work for Parents in High-Conflict

Upon first hearing about the Child Support Account, most think it is a reasonable option for cooperative parents who have had some moderate success at joint decision-making. However, the skeptics ask, "What about those parents who seem to fight all the time?" Or, "You must be kidding! You clearly haven't met the person I was married to for the past 18 years!" Or, "How could it possibly work where one or both of the parents are high-conflict personality types? Aren't you just setting them up for failure?" And, perhaps the most compelling skeptic's statement: "You really don't understand, the reason we got divorced is we could never agree on *anything!*"

Here are a few of the reasons why the Account seems to work so well, even for high-conflict couples:

IT CHANGES THE FOCUS TO THEIR CHILDREN

The Child Support Account shifts the focus of both parents from each other to their children's needs. Engaging in the joint task of deciding on their children's budget, discussing whether certain children's expenses can be afforded, and seeing their child support money go *directly* to the needs of their children somehow have a transforming effect on even the most toxic of parents.[33] The process of using this Account imposes a reality check on parents who would otherwise remaining struggling with each other.

In the mediation room, we often say to the challenging parents: "Well, I think you only have two choices; you can do this stuff yourselves, or somebody else will do it for you, and at great expense. I can help you build a budget covering all the costs for your children's food, health care, clothing, activity fees, tutoring, enrichment, and any other expenses of your children that you would like to include and share. Or, you can walk into a court room and be given some magical number– the amount that one of you will be ordered to pay to the other for child support. This magical number will have been arrived at through a formula that some economist suggested is the average cost of raising children, determined by statistics from the Department of Agriculture and by consumer expenditure surveys produced by the Bureau of Labor Statistics. When faced with two choices: deciding for yourselves or having someone else decide for you, most parents opt for self-empowerment. *You can decide the child support amount and method you wish to use, or the state will do it for you–IT'S YOUR CHOICE."*

IT CREATES STRUCTURE

We know that people in conflict benefit from structure.[34] Interactions between parents in high conflict are often chaotic. Using the Child Support Guidelines, a judge will order a lump-sum amount of monthly child support, with no structure or guidance as to how it will be used. This amount is often called "basic support," "family support," or just plain "child support." Traditionally, courts have avoided the detail-work of budgeting, and they do not create orders telling parents how each child support dollar should be spent. This is understandable because it is easier to give dollars to one parent and say, "You're the better parent (think custodial parent), so *you* decide how to spend it." Even though the Guideline's approach produces conflict over what the basic support should cover, from the court's point of view it is certainly more cost-effective to give the custodial parent authority to manage child support than hiring more judges to commence budgeting hearings.

Even if the support amount is accepted by the parent who pays, parents in high conflict will still fight over which expenses of the children the support payment should be used for. This lack of structure is resolved when parents create an itemized budget of what a support dollar should cover. *You can jointly decide what your child support should be used for, or you can engage in a custody battle to determine who gets to decide how to spend support dollars– IT'S YOUR CHOICE.*

IT UTILIZES THE "FAIRNESS PRINCIPLE"

Use of the Child Support Account allows parents to see that they each are equivalently carrying the costs of child-rearing. When building the budget of children's expenses together, parents consider whether the items being discussed are necessary and affordable. At the conclusion of this budget discussion, parents then decide whether to share children's expenses equally, or proportionally, in which case the higher-income parent contributes more to the Account. At this point, they are faced with considering what we call the "Fairness Principle."

This fairness principle, regarding proportional contributions, arises from the general concept common to all state Guidelines, that the higher-income parent should contribute more to the costs of raising their children than should the lower-income parent. When a parent disagrees with this concept and demands equal contributions to the Account by both parents, we find that there is usually a perception by the higher-income parent that the lower-income parent is not earning up to his or her full potential. That is, the higher-income parent may believe that the other parent should be working more hours or finding a higher-paying job. Regardless, we have found that the vast majority of parents readily agree to the inherent fairness of setting contributions to the Child Support Account on a proportional basis, according to their gross incomes.

In adversarial divorces, where the parents are represented by aggressively advocating attorneys, parents will often spend a great deal of time trying to prove that their opponent is under-reporting income. There may be an allegation that one of them has come down with the disease of "Low-Income Syndrome (LIS)" which, reportedly, seems to strike self-employed people in the first year of their divorce! A good option for resolution is to appoint a CPA or a CFP (Certified Financial Planner) to serve as a neutral expert to look over tax returns or business income from various sources, with the goal of recommending a fair income number to use when income sources are complex or intermittent. In fact, this procedure for using a neutral can routinely be written into the Child Support Account language as a mechanism for settling future disputes regarding the determination of income.

While state Guidelines generally follow the principle that, whoever earns more should pay more to the children, a minority of parents deviate from this and decide to share 50/50 for all agreed-upon children's expenses, regardless of who makes more or less. These parents agree to always follow a principle of 50/50 sharing. They tend be large-asset, high-income parents, who may have a variety of sources of income, including commissions, bonuses and other investments, that enable both parents to fund agreed-upon children's expenses, regardless of income swings each year. However, when average-income parents have conflict and one demands that there always be exactly equal contributions, this is usually because one parent thinks that the other is not carrying his or her fair share, due to underemployment, or working part-time. In such cases, the mediator can help the parents discuss ways for increasing incomes, decreasing expenses, or for finding other ways to achieve a mutual sense of balance and fairness.

The court system handles this particular issue through the concept of "imputed income." When hearings are held, expert witnesses present conflicting testimony about what the less-income parent should be earning. We have seen many cases in mediation in which the fees for the experts used to fight lengthy court battles over the amount of his income could have been used to fund all of the remaining years of child support, had the money not been used to pay for litigation expenses billed by the experts and the attorneys on both sides.

You can decide on your own mutual sense of fairness, or you can appear in court and be told about the state's standard of fairness that you must follow– IT'S YOUR CHOICE.

IT REDUCES THE TENDENCY TO BLAME AND FIND FAULT

The tendency for one parent to blame the other parent for actions and events in the past is significantly reduced or eliminated because the focus of the Account is mostly on the future. There is no need to calculate a Guidelines amount, based upon who has had the children most in the past, because in developing and using the Account, time spent with their children in the past is irrelevant.

In those cases in which the more-time parent has more expenses, due to feeding them more often, and driving them to more activities, an additional amount for those expenses can be taken from the shared-cost budget items, and used by the more-time parent. Unhooking time from the support amount removes the need to engage in blame and fault, because blame and fault are the currency used in trying to reach a particular custody outcome. When pursuing a particular custody label to obtain more child support, the strategy for winning is to show that the other parent is less worthy of being with their children, which always generates blame and fault. *You can engage in fault-finding to better your chance at winning custody, or you can let your children enjoy both of their parents, by use of the Child Support Account–IT'S YOUR CHOICE.*

IT ALLOWS FOR COMPARTMENTALIZATION

We will borrow a psychological concept, called "compartmentalization." This means, simply, that people are often able to separate and isolate inconsistent feelings and beliefs, in order to avoid discomfort or mental anguish. Because the Child Support Account funnels child support funds directly to the children and not through the hands of only one parent, it is possible for parents to continue to harbor deep anger towards each other while, at the same time, scrupulously adhering to the rules created for using the Child Support Account. Compartmentalization may be a useful concept to explain why certain parents, such as those who we might describe as high-conflict people or those who are unable to fully accept the reality of the divorce and move on with their lives, can still successfully join with the other parent to effectively use the Child Support Account.

When the recipient of child support is resented by the paying parent, the children often get caught in the crossfire. However, in spite of parents being in toxic, emotional conflict with one another, their children can still be loved, protected, and provided for through the use of the Child Support Account, if the parents create a firm boundary between their anger toward each other and their desire to do what is right for their children. *You can let the anger spill over to your children, or you can use the Child Support Account as tool to separate the business of parenting from your unresolved grief and anger over the divorce– IT'S YOUR CHOICE.*

MUTUAL-THINKING IS MORE LIKELY TO BE CREATED

Use of the Child Support Account helps each parent to realize that in order for one to get a good, fair, and just result, the other parent must also be able to obtain a good, fair, and just result. The Child Support Account avoids courthouse rules of contested engagement, which results in winners and losers. Only one parent gets his or her needs met when everything is framed in terms of who pays and who receives money, who gets custody, and who becomes a *visiting parent.* In our efforts in Minnesota to achieve passage of the Minnesota Private Cooperative Divorce Bill,[35] we have testified repeatedly that parents need an option to opt out of the contest system of the Court and negotiate for their needs and interests, rather than fight over winning and losing. Use of the Child Support Account requires joint discussion. It will not work for either parent unless it works for both parents. It is as if some sort of synergy is created by using the Account that leads to greater cooperation. *One of you can prevail over the other, or you BOTH can win– IT'S YOUR CHOICE.*

RESULTS

Recently, a Dad in our office had just agreed to contribute to the Child Support Account $375 per month more than the Guidelines would have required him to send to Mom. We asked him what his response will be when his attorney says to him, "I could have gotten you a much lower child support payment." He responded: "Here is what I am going to tell him–'I can find 150 divorced dads within a ten-mile radius of this office who have child support withheld from their check twice a month, who would give their right arm to have what I have'." He continued, "With the Child Support Account, I have a wife who is not playing the custody card, just to get more money from me, a wife who is willing to agree to equivalent time-sharing of our children, and a wife who is not demanding that the support and collections office create a nightmare for me and for the bookkeeper where I work. I have an arrangement where I get to see how every dollar of child support that I deposit into the Account is spent. When my kid asks me for money for something, I don't have to say, 'Get it from Mom, because that's what my child support is for.' Instead, I can say, 'Let me pay for it out of the Child Support Account, because being a parent is also buying things for you, son. Now, let's go get what you need.'"

Likewise, a Mom sitting in our office was once asked what she might say if her attorney was skeptical about using the Child Support Account. She said, "I will tell my attorney that, for some time, I have been trying to get the kid's dad to buy things for them. I need his help. I am tired of trying to make do with what is available, and then getting grief from him because we do not have enough money to put the kids into every sport he wants them to be in, or to go to every camp they wish to attend. Now, more than ever, he will see and understand what it really costs to raise our children."

The message to those who find themselves in angry, highly-conflicted, co-parenting relationships: "You can go to court and receive the Guidelines child support order, and the court's support and collections apparatus, and have your custody trial, or you can voluntarily try to use the Child Support Account. It may be your first area of success together. If it does not work for either one of you, all you need to say is, "I want to stop using this, because it is not working for us." *You can try to make it work and reap the benefits, or you can have support and collections do the work for you—IT'S YOUR CHOICE.*

Chapter Ten:

Some Final Words to Help You Get Started

Calculating Child Support Guidelines Using a Worksheet or Website

The Federal Court System has shied away from getting involved in the messy business of divorce and has left divorce procedures and divorce laws to the various states, resulting in wide variations among the states. As you proceed with seeking approval by the court for using the Child Support Account, it is necessary for you to check your own state statutes, regarding two items:

1) Try to find a website or, at the very least, a state published worksheet that helps you calculate your state's version of the support Guidelines; and,

2) Try to find, and read through, your own state's Guidelines regarding what is required to be asserted in your documents to achieve approval for deviating from child support Guidelines.

You can contact a local family law attorney, professional family mediator, paralegal or court-related family law facilitator, to assist you in obtaining this information.

If you are parents who have never married and have decided to live apart, you may freely use the language of the Child Support Account, as outlined in this book because you are not seeking court approval for your separation arrangements. Most importantly, you will *not* need to appear in court because you are not seeking to end a state-licensed, approved marriage. And, since you do not need the court's help to award custody or find an absent parent who should be assisting in support of a child or children, you do not need to concern yourselves with Guidelines or deviation criteria.

However, if you are commencing a lawsuit in order to terminate the contract of marriage, you should be able to find information about your own state's child support guideline calculator by using a search engine to find the appropriate website. You will find that many states provide a website Guidelines calculator that allows you to type in income, number of children, and other information required to calculate support. If you happen to live in the state of Minnesota, you will find it at: https://childsupportcalculator.dhs.state.mn.us. It is the authorized, state-approved Guidelines child support calculator.

When the federal government did dip its toe into the murky waters of divorce, it did so to create a better system for tracking down and obtaining money from those absent parents who abandoned their children, causing the state to use tax dollars to care for their children in the form of Welfare or TANF payments paid to the remaining parent. The Family Support Act of 1988, which has been discussed above, allowed each state to create its own child support Guidelines formulas (which is why each state has different Guidelines), and it further empowered each state to establish its own rules for allowing for deviations from the Guidelines.

Just as we urge you to locate your state Guidelines, using any search engine, you also can find web pages that address what must be asserted in order to deviate from the Guidelines. If you cannot find any information, or, if your state court does not have helpful websites, you can always rely on the initiating language of the Family Support Act as interpreted by the Federal Office of Child Support and Enforcement, which, in part, states: "While the standard guideline calculation addresses the basic needs of a child, deviation criteria tailor the order to meet the needs of a specific child or children, therefore, we have agreed to use the Child Support Account to tailor our child support plan to specifically meet the diverse and changing needs of our children." (see footnote 28 on page 61)

You also might want to use the following paragraph, if you are unsure of specific language to use. Feel free to add it to the end of the sample language in the Appendix:

> The budget included herein addresses the basic needs of our child (ren) and is also specifically tailored to meet the special and extraordinary needs of the child(ren)," as opposed to using the Guidelines formula that combines our child(ren)'s expense needs with every other child in the state to create a single formulaic result that may not provide individual fairness to our children.

In the final analysis, you may need to go to your courthouse and ask the facilitator at the Self-Help Desk or a judge's clerk for what your assigned judge needs to see in the document that you submit to the court. For example, California and Arizona expect you to include language that says your deviation from the Guidelines amount is voluntary and not based upon coercion. Other states seem to want you to explain why a deviation is in the "best interests" of the minor child or children.

Finally, what follows is a complete set of all the previously presented, essential separate paragraphs of the Child Support Account. This set of paragraphs would be everything needed to be included in a normal filing with the court, to accomplish a request to deviate from the Guidelines and permit use of the Child Support Account. You also may need to find out about other customary local requirements that might be necessary to address in the child support section. For example, Minnesota expects that marital termination agreements also contain agreements that reflect decisions concerning funding of child support with life insurance, if life insurance was a part of the marital finances. Some states expect you to decide who will claim the children as exemptions in the future and who will be claiming Head of Household tax filing status. These are all governed by local jurisdictional rules and with a little assistance, you should be able to obtain guidance about the relevant information on those important details (These may seem like housekeeping matters, but, in reality, funding child support with life insurance and addressing how to cooperate around tax deductions/exemptions relating to the children, are standard and important parts of marital termination agreements).

COMPLETE SAMPLE CHILD SUPPORT ACCOUNT PARAGRAPHS IN ONE PLACE, IN THE ORDER IN WHICH YOU WOULD LIKELY USE THEM:

You will, of course, insert your own numbers and other personal information, to create a children's budget of expenses to use in your particular state, and reflecting your own, unique situation.

> Amount of **(Insert Your State)** Guidelines Support. The parents have determined the **(Your State)** Child Support Guidelines would require Mother to pay Father the approximate sum of $164 per month for child support, which is based upon the following:
>
> 1) Father earns $65,000 gross income per year ($5,417

gross per month); and Mother earns $39,000 gross income per year ($3,250 gross per month); and

2) Father and Mother are not exchanging spousal maintenance; and

3) Father pays for the children's health insurance premiums in the amount of $234 per month, and for the dental insurance premiums in the amount of $13 per month, included in the above sum; and

4) Mother and Father have no daycare costs for their children; and

5) Mother and Father are following an approximately equivalent, time-sharing parenting schedule.

However, Father and Mother will not be following the Guidelines and instead, have agreed to an arrangement for sharing the costs of raising their children that calls for itemizing all expenses related to their children, in the amount of $1,258 per month, and sharing these costs on a pro-rata basis according to their gross annual incomes. This amount will be calculated on the basis of determining the percentage of their respective gross annual incomes in relation to their combined gross annual income. Father's gross income is $65,000 per year, and Mother's gross income is $39,000 per year. Mother earns 37% of their combined total income, and she agrees to pay $465 each month into the joint account; Father earns 63% of their combined total incomes, and he agrees to pay $791 each month into the joint account. This $791 includes $234 of health insurance for the minor children deducted from Father's salary, and $557 cash paid into the Account by Father, for a total contribution of $791 each month.

Therefore, each parent shall contribute towards the below-listed expenses of their children, set forth in the "shared" column below, by depositing these amounts monthly into a children's joint account, and the itemized "shared" expenses below shall be paid by either parent from that Account.

AUTHORITY FOR DEVIATION: (Minnesota State Parenting Plan legislation [518.1705 Subd. 8) states that "**(a)** parents creating a parenting plan are subject to the requirements of the child support Guidelines under Chapter 518A," and that "**(b)** parents may include in the parenting plan an allocation of expenses for the child(ren). The allocation is an enforceable contract between the parents.

AUTHORITY FOR DEVIATION: (In other states) Federal Regulations created as a result of the Family Support Act of 1988 allow for deviations to address the special needs of our children. The budget included herein addresses not only the basic needs of our child(ren), but is also specifically tailored to meet the special and extraordinary needs of the child(ren). The Guidelines formula that combines our child(ren) with every other child in the state into one formulaic child support result is unlikely to provide fairness to our children or to our family, now residing in two separate households. Therefore, we parents, together, respectfully request that the court approve our use of the Child Support Account as described more fully below.

The parents prefer to use this method of sharing the costs of raising their children, instead of one parent sending a sum of money to the other, because this sharing of children's costs:

(a) Permits both parents to pay for items that their children need when their children are with that parent, instead of telling their children they must ask the recipient of child support to always purchase necessary items for them; and

(b) Provides a record of expenses incurred by their children or on their behalf, thereby allowing the parents to more easily make future modifications of the child support as their children's expenses change in the future; and

(c) Does not tie child support to time with their children, thereby separating the parenting time discussions from its effect on the amount of child support exchanged; and

(d) Allows for periodic adjustments to child support by modifying the amount deposited into the Account from each parent upon review of changes to each parent's income;

(e) Is a continuation of the joint consultation and decision-making that naturally takes place between the parents during their marriage (and/or during their separation);

(f) Is consistent with the parents' choice to mediate their divorce, which is evidenced by their shared parenting plan that requires them to share (proportionally or equally) in the future costs of raising their children.

The parents believe it is in their children's best interests to reserve the issue of one parent paying child support to the other, and, instead, to require the sharing of expenses as provided herein.

There are no arrearages in child support as of the date of the final hearing. The parents intend to use a joint account to manage and disburse the funds necessary for payment of the "shared" children's expenses. Separate expenses to be paid by each parent directly and not from the joint account are also set forth below. The following represents a sample of an "initial budget of expenses," and the parents expect that, from time to time, they will meet and review or adjust these expense estimates.

Table 10-1. Children's Monthly Expenses

Expense Item	Paid Separately by Dad	Shared	Paid Separately by Mom
Food and groceries	250		250
Eating out	150		150
Lunches at School		85	
Clothing		110	
Cell Phones		60	
Medical Insurance for the two children [If deducted from a paycheck, show who pays]	Deducted from Dad's paycheck	234	
Uncovered medical		34	
Uncovered dental		5	
Uncovered medication prescriptions		20	
Orthodontia		0	
Eyeglasses/Contact Lenses		35	
Car Insurance - daughter		110	
Dance (Costumes/Competition Costs)		250	
School Supplies & Backpacks		20	
Tutoring		127	
Sports (Soccer equipment, fees, and camp)		69	
Haircuts/ Hair Care		40	
Personal care items (cosmetics/other drugstore items)		45	
Gifts for friends' birthday parties		12	
TOTAL Expenses Anticipated to be Paid Separately by Each Parent: [Paid from their own separate funds]	400		400
TOTAL Shared Expenses for their children: [Items with a zero are also considered shared]		1,256	
Shared Costs Paid by Each [63%-37%]: [For example, if Dad earns $65k annual income and Mom earns $39k annual income, Dad's 63% of $1,256 is $791, and Mom's 37% of $1,256 is $465	791		465
Medical Insurance Paid Directly by Dad: [This is reimbursed to Dad, by subtracting it from his 63%, because he pays it directly through paychecks, and it is included in his contribution to the shared column]	-234		
Monthly Amount Deposited into Account by Each:	557		465

Each parent shall pay separately for food, recreation, entertainment and travel expenses, which will not be shared as a part of the joint account arrangement.

From time to time, and at least once every 12 months, the parents will meet and review the budgeted expenses for their children. At such review, they may add new categories of expenses and may revise current expenditure levels. Upon a substantial change in either of their incomes, they shall also adjust their pro-rata contributions to the Account. In February of each year, they will exchange W-2 income verification or tax returns in order to adjust their pro-rata contribution towards their children's joint account. Should there be any dispute about the amounts of their respective current gross incomes, they will submit the dispute to a mutually agreed upon C.P.A. or professional family mediator.

Mom and Dad agree that neither will spend from the joint account for items other than the above authorized categories. Should there be extraordinary and unusual expenses for their children that have not been anticipated and not part of their projected expenses, they agree first to meet and discuss whether or not to incur the expense, and if they agree, the item will be paid from the joint account.

In the event that either parent determines that the joint account becomes impractical, or is working unsatisfactorily, that parent may declare that this arrangement be terminated. They shall

```
then first return to mediation, or, in the event
mediation does not result in agreement, to court,
in order to establish a different child support
arrangement.
```

Conclusion

If you are impatient with the pace of reforms occurring in the court system, you do have a choice. You now have the ability to create a better system. You can join with your child(ren)'s other parent to create a fairer child support process, by using the Child Support Account and adhering to its terms.

By doing so, you and your children's other parent will be creating and abiding by your own, shared concepts of fairness. You do not need to wait for your state legislature to act in order to give you permission to use the Child Support Account. You can immediately step out of the dangerous undertow of custody battles, costly court fights, and endless conflict by using the Account now.

When you use the Child Support Account, you will find it easier to view the other parent as your parenting partner. You will find that, by choosing to use the Child Support Account, you can begin to let go of rights and wrongs, wins and losses, and the pain and hurt that come with that way of thinking. You can, indeed, give your children a better future. We hope you do!

Best wishes for the journey ahead.

Footnotes

[1] Timothy Grall, *Custodial Mothers and Fathers and Their Child Support: 2013* Issued January 2016, in Current Population Reports, United States Census Bureau, at www.census.gov/content/dam/Census/library/publications/2016/demo/P60-255.pdf

[2] Joey Arthur, *Trends In Child Support Debt Amounts,* Blog, Office of Child Support and Enforcement, March 15, 2018 at www.acf.hhs.gov/css/ocsedatablog/2018/3/trends-in-child-support-amount. Last visited 03/25/2019.

[3] In this book, we refer to the term, "Professional Family Mediator." For information about these divorce professionals, we encourage you to read the *Standards of Practice for Professional Family Mediators* at one of the following websites: https://apfmnet.org/standards-practice-professional-family-mediators/, or www.professionalmediatorcertification.com. For help locating a Professional Family Mediator, go to the Academy of Professional Family Mediators website at apfmnet.org.

[4] Joey Arthur, *Trends In Child Support Debt Amounts,* Blog, Office of Child Support and Enforcement, March 15, 2018 at www.acf.hhs.gov/css/ocsedatablog/2018/3/trends-in-child-support-amount. Last visited 03/25/2019.

[5] Douglas Galbi, quoted in Prison Legal News, September 2, 2016. https://www.prisonlegalnews.org/news/2016/sep/2/poor-parents-fail-pay-child-support-go-jail. See also Frances Robles and Shalia Dewan, *Skip Child Support. Go to Jail. Lose Job. Repeat,* New York Times, April 19, 2015. https://www.nytimes.com/2015/04/20/us/skip-child-support-go-to-jail-repeat last visited 07/15/2018.

[6] *Minnesota Statutes* 518.1705 Parenting Plan Act

[7] Interview with former MN House of Representatives legislator Andy Dawkins 7-1-18, Chief Author of Minnesota Parenting Plan legislation.

[8] "As advocate, a lawyer zealously asserts the client's position under the rules of the adversary system." Preamble, *Minnesota Rules of Professional Conduct*, Effective Oct 1, 2005 with amendments through July 1, 2018. at http://lprb.mncourts.gov/rules/Documents/MN%20Rules%20of%20Professional%20Conduct.pdf.

[9] *See, generally,* Scott Altman, *Lurking in the Shadows*, 68 S. Cal. L. Rev.493, (1995) (discussing the problem of trading days for dollars).

[10] Family Support Act of 1988 (Pub.L. 100–485, 102 Stat. 2343, enacted October 13, 1988).

[11] Office of Child Support Enforcement, US Department of Health Human Services https://www.acf.hhs.gov/css/parents/what-happens-if-child-support-isnt-paid (last visited 7-15-18) Page one

[12] Judges can use their inherent contempt powers, because not paying child support is akin to challenging the court's authority.

[13] For larger arrearages over a certain amount in child support, one can be convicted for felony criminal non-support in some states.

[14] To determine whether a state charges interest on child support arrears, please go to your state court's website, or check with the State Office of Support and Collections.

[15] Joey Arthur, *Trends In Child Support Debt Amounts*, Blog, Office of Child Support and Enforcement, March 15, 2018 at www.acf.hhs.gov/css/ocsedatablog/2018/3/trends-in-child-support-amount. last visited 6-18-28. Also see: Scott Hargreaves, CNN Money, November 5, 2012 at www.money.cnn/2012/11/05/news/economy/unpaid-child-support

[16] Douglas Galbi, https://www.prisonlegalnews.org/news/2016/sep/2/poor-parents-fail-pay-child-support-go-jail; see also Frances Robles and Shalia Dewan, *Skip Child Support. Go to Jail. Lose Job. Repeat,* New York Times, April 19, 2015. https://www.nytimes.com/2015/04/20/us/skip-child-support-go-to-jail-repeat last visited 7-15-18.

[17] For example, Wisconsin Child Support Guidelines calculate the non-custodial parent's child support on a sliding scale that calls for 17% of gross income for one child, 25% of gross for two children, 29% of gross income for three children, 31% of gross income for four children and 34% of gross income for five or more children. The custodial parent's income is not considered. However, under an income shares model, such as in Minnesota, both parents' incomes will affect the amount of child support paid by one parent to the other. https://dcf.wisconsin.gov/cs/order/guidelines

[18] Bill Doherty, Testimony in support of HF 1115, Minnesota House of Representatives, Civil Law hearing on "Minnesota Cooperative Private Divorce Bill," April 7, 2019.

[19] To find a professional family mediator near you who is knowledgeable about the use of the Child Support Account, and can provide assistance and referral, go to www.thechildsupportaccount.com

[20] For comparison purposes, using the above income example in Minnesota,: If the parents were following an equal time-sharing arrangement, and health insurance for the two children is paid by Father, he would be required to send to Mother $144 per month as child support, using the Minnesota Child Support Calculator, found at https://childsupportcalculator.dhs.state.mn.us. As in the above Child Support Account example, it is not unusual for the higher-earning parent to contribute more towards the children's expenses than the child support guidelines would require. Here, Father is contributing $791 per month to the account, and Mother's is contributing $465 per month to the account. By using the Child Support Account, they also have created agreements about sharing extracurricular sports, dance, car insurance and tutoring costs, which, under existing guidelines, often generate conflict, because such extra expenses are not part of the guidelines' computations.

[21] Bird nesting is an arrangement in which their children continue to reside in the family home after the parents separate or divorce, and the parents alternate moving in and out of the home. Each parent separately resides in the family home for agreed upon periods of time, e.g. a week at a time. Such an arrangement is usually transitional, and used only until two suitable residences are established by the parents.

[22] In Minnesota, for example, you can find it at https://childsupportcalculator.dhs.state.mn.us/

[23] In Duluth, Minnesota, for example, the self-help desk for St. Louis County is located in the law library of the courthouse, on the ground floor. They will give you legal *information* (but not legal *advice*) and will help you understand how the Minnesota Child Support Calculator works. Most states have this type of assistance, due to the increasing number of self-represented families. All of them, of course, must refrain from giving you legal advice, which is usually defined as predicting how a judge will rule after hearing the facts of your particular case.

[24] For more detailed information about using budgets in divorce planning, see *Mediating Divorce: A Step-By-Step Manual,* 1999, by Marilyn S. McKnight and Stephen K. Erickson. San Francisco: Jossey-Bass Publishers, 75-88.

[25] "Arrearages" is a term used to describe unpaid child support that is still owed under a previous court order. If you are converting from Guidelines child support to the Child Support Account, both parents would need to assert that there is no outstanding, unpaid child support at the time of the request to deviate.

[26] The Guidelines were mandated by Congress in 1988 to solve the problem of collecting child support from an "absent parent" (see Family Support Act of 1988 (Pub.L. 100–485, 102 Stat. 2343, enacted October 13, 1988). Here, you are assuring the court that you will not abandon your children, thereby causing the state to pay for raising them. You will always submit to the Guidelines' requirements if the Child Support Account fails to work for you. Therefore, when you agree that the court may reserve the issue, you tell the judge that you are willing to put the Guidelines on the back shelf, and, in the event you choose to end use of the Child Support Account, then the court reserves the right to impose the Guidelines in the future, if necessary.

[27] U.S. Department of Health and Human Services, Office of Child Support Enforcement, Resource Library, Essentials for Attorneys in Child [Support] Enforcement, 3rd Edition, Chapter 9, page 166 at https://www.acf.hhs.gov/sites/default/files/programs/css/essentials_for_attorneys_ch09.pdf.

[28] AUTHORITY FOR DEVIATION: Minnesota State Parenting Plan legislation [518.1705 Subd. 8 states that "(a) parents creating a parenting plan are subject to the requirements of the child support guidelines under Chapter 518A," and that "(b) parents may include in the parenting plan an allocation of expenses for their children. The allocation is an enforceable contract between the parents. "

[29] Interview with Molly Olson, 10-15-19, Child Reform advocate and speaker on IV D collection programs.

[30] See Code of Federal Regulations, Title 45 section 305.2 Performance Measures:

[31] https://www.acf.hhs.gov/sites/default/files/programs/css/essentials_for_attorneys_ch09.pdf. Page 166

[32] In 1998, Marilyn McKnight and Steve Erickson invited a group of therapists, attorneys, mediators, legislators and others to form an ad hoc group to explore passage of parenting plan legislation, in an effort to change the frame from battling over custody to building parenting plans. Nine of us emerged as the core of the group, and we spent the next three years working to obtain passage of the bill in 2001. See Minnesota Parenting Plan. MSA 518.175 subd. 8

[33] See Bill Eddy (at www.highconflictinstitute.com), co-founder of the High Conflict Institute, for further information about managing high-conflict personalities. Bill Eddy, and his numerous books on shifting high-conflict people from blaming and fault-finding to logical thinking, stress the need for structure. Indeed, his work has reaffirmed the beneficial result of helping people to shift from fixating on the past to working out a plan for the future. Even high-conflict personality types will be compelled to change their primitive fight-or-flight thinking to more logical problem-solving, when provided with a structure that mutually engages the parents.

[34] See Bill Eddy https://www.highconflictinstitute.com.

[35] Minnesota Cooperative Private Divorce Bill, (as of April 21, 2019, found as House File 1115, currently in conference committee and awaiting a full floor vote).

Made in the USA
Las Vegas, NV
15 January 2021